Paid to Be Perfect

THE SECRET TO FINDING YOUR PERFECT

Paid to Be Perfect

THE SECRET TO FINDING YOUR PERFECT

Heather Mathes

gatekeeper press™
Columbus, Ohio

Paid to Be Perfect: Fit Model Secrets to Find Your Perfect

Published by Gatekeeper Press
2167 Stringtown Rd, Suite 109
Columbus, OH 43123-2989
www.GatekeeperPress.com

The interior formatting, typesetting, and editorial work for this book are entirely the product of the author. Gatekeeper Press did not participate in and is not responsible for any aspect of these elements.

Library of Congress Control Number: 2021943218

ISBN (hardcover): 9781662923517
ISBN (paperback): 9781662916991
eISBN: 9781662917004

Disclaimer and Words of Caution

Before starting any new diet and exercise program, please check with your doctor to clear any diet or exercise changes. The author is NOT a doctor, nutritionist, or registered dietitian. This book is not intended as a substitute for professional medical advice, diagnosis, or treatment. The reader should regularly consult a physician in matters relating to their health and particularly with respect to any symptoms that may require diagnosis or medical attention. Never disregard professional medical advice or delay seeking it because of something you have read in this book. Individual results are not guaranteed and may vary.

A Note About Eating Disorders

Eating disorders are complex mental and physical illnesses that can affect people of all body types, genders, ages, races, religions, ethnicities, sexual orientations, and weights. If you find that you are struggling with obsessive or compulsive thoughts and behaviors about your body, eating, or exercise, please consult a licensed therapist as these may be symptoms of an eating disorder. For more information about what an eating disorder is and how to access treatment, please check out the following web resources:

www.nationaleatingdisorders.org

www.allianceforeatingdisorders.com/what-are-eating-disorders

Acknowledgements:

For the one who inspired my love of fashion-my mom, Barbara.
For the one who inspired my love of writing-my dad, Larry.
For the one who has co-written this journey through life with me-my husband, Jeff.
For the one who writes the future-our son, Luc.

With special thanks to all the people who have helped me along the way to finding my own perfect, and to the one who had a spark of inspiration with which I created a flame, my human body twin "T".

Contents

x

Per.fect
/perfikt/

adjective

Having all the required or desirable elements, qualities, or characteristics; as good as it is possible to be. - Oxford Languages[1]

---

1 Oxford University Press (2021), Lexico, s.v. "perfect."

Introduction

I am a body twin-a nearly identical match-to a lifeless mannequin form that clothing manufacturers use to make clothes fit in mass retail. Being measured and discovered to match measurements and body type to the fit form I've modeled alongside throughout the years was how I became paid to be "perfect." We-the form and I-measure the same on most measurements from our head circumference to our ankles. And I've maintained my body measurements under contract from my 20s to my late 40s, within tolerance of plus or minus a quarter of an inch.

My stories are based on these experiences working in the fashion industry as a model and specializing as a standard size six contemporary fit model-a niche in the world of fashion modeling-to show you exactly how (other than during pregnancy and shortly thereafter) I have kept my body at the same measurements while eating whatever I want, without stress or guilt.

Whether you're a size 2 or 22, know that what I share can be applied to ANY and ALL sizes and shapes as well as ages. The message beyond the fit model statistics (provided throughout for context) is body positivity for everybody and every *body*.

To achieve consistency your measurements and weight will not be absolutely exact from day to day. There is a range on the scale of a little bit bigger and a little bit smaller that we all vacillate between as absolute exact weights and measurements are not humanly possible. The point is to eliminate the extremes as well as to find pleasure in the one thing you will do every day you're on this beautiful earth: eat.

Consistency is only one part of the story. True contentment and happiness will never be found in a number on a scale. Though having the knowledge to naturally create this consistency is freedom-freedom to NOT obsess about your weight so that you have time to focus on all the best that life has in store for you. If that's your goal, you're in the right place.

The first section, Part One: The Secret to Finding Your Perfect, provides a glimpse into the world of fit modeling to explain how I came to the knowledge around consistency of my own weight and measurements and how that led to what I do today. I then dive deep into all of my nutrition, fitness, skin care and wellness methods to help those of all ages and sizes find their own perfect.

Part Two: The Fit Model Manual, shares detailed insider information for those who dream of getting into the business and ask, "How can I become a fit model?" I reveal how I got my big break into modeling and everything I've learned about the business throughout the years while working under contract with a major national retailer. This manual is my pay-it-forward for the amazing career I've been fortunate to have had over my decades-long modeling career.

Before I begin, know that my way is one way, but there are many other routes to take. You may align with me 100%, or you may take a little from my story, or you may have your own completely unique path to follow. Whichever path you take, this book is about using my stories to work with what Mother Nature gave YOU to be your best self and find YOUR PERFECT-yours alone which may be altogether different from the "perfect" I share here.

And while I have been paid to be "perfect," I am NOT perfect. What does that even mean anyway-to be perfect? Think for a minute of how miraculous it is that we are even here on this planet. How often do we think about the fact that we are hurtling through space while our beautiful earth journeys around the sun right at this very moment as we go about our day-to-day lives? Or how amazing it is that our various ancestors' fastest sperm made their way to each egg, creating each generation of us in perfection? Despite the first line of this paragraph, all of us, here, now are perfect simply because we exist.

The contradiction occurs because we generally think of the word perfect in the way of flaws, which of course everyone has, and I am no exception. This book is not about striving to be absolutely perfect-a thing which does not exist. Instead it's about helping you find or fine-tune your own unique path that only you can create-the path that's perfect for *you*. It's about making mistakes along the way without judging ourselves because that's how we learn, grow, and truly discover what perfect looks like in our own lives. It's about appreciating those inevitable bumps in the road, knowing that the growth will fuel our ever-evolving potential. It's about acceptance of wherever you land in life, knowing deep down that it's all a part of the process. Even when you don't particularly like where you are, that feeling that something is "off" is the only way to become aware that it's time to make some changes.

So yes, it's technically true that nobody is perfect. However the dichotomy remains that it's also true that we are ALL perfect exactly as we are, exactly where we should be, at exactly the right time. And maybe this book landed in your hands at the perfect time for you!

PART ONE:
THE SECRET TO FINDING YOUR PERFECT

Chapter 1 - **What is a Fit Model?**

So what exactly is a fit model and why should you care? Good questions.

A career modeling in the fashion industry is a well-known career choice but fit modeling to most people outside of the fashion world is a mystery. When I've said "I'm a fit model" I've had to spell it out F-I-T numerous times because they often think I'm saying "foot model." Maybe they've heard of hand models and that creates the confusion. Perhaps I don't say "fit" clearly enough. Or both.

People also sometimes assume a fit model is a fitness model. They think it has something to do with strength or bodybuilding. It doesn't. Although I do work out regularly, that is not a part of the actual job while fit modeling.

Another common misconception is that because I'm a model I'm walking runways and doing photoshoots regularly, neither of which describes the work of a fit model accurately. Though I have done plenty of runway shows throughout the years and I have found myself in front of the camera in photo shoots even in my semi-retirement. In any case I'm not a size zero, I am not six feet tall, and I don't have to be in the age range of 14 to 25 to get booked.

So what then is a fit model? The easiest way to explain the work of a fit model is to think of a live walking/ talking mannequin that is required to maintain their body measurements in order to help standardize the fit of a clothing brand. We work with pattern makers, designers, clothing merchandisers, and technical coordinators to check the fit, drape, and visual appearance of a design on a real human being before the garment goes into mass production. This helps to ensure the perfect fit of a clothing line. The size made to fit the model is essentially couture for the model fitting the garment which then gets mathematically graded up and down to all the other sizes.

In essence, a fit model is a specialized model that has "perfect" proportions within a framework of what is desired by a certain company. We fulfill the standard body measurements that the fashion brand wants to use to base their fit from. And we need to know exactly what we measure and how we compare to the form.

The life of a fit model involves a lot of standing, a lot of pinning, and most importantly, the model's measurements must stay consistent throughout the whole design, pattern-making, and production process. That consistency still allows for a "tolerance"-a measurement that is a little higher or a little lower than the baseline of what our target specifications are. That tolerance is built into our contracts because it's impossible not to change slightly from day to day. But being "within tolerance" of your normal is easily manageable not only for fit models but for all of us if we are at our natural size.

In the opposite way that you would think, fit modeling kills your insecurity about most of your physical imperfections because knowing your "flaws" is also a part of the job. We see our imperfections regularly in a room full of people under bright, fluorescent lights as they are highlighted and scrutinized in comparison to an actual perfect, static form. (I honestly can't even begin to guess how many hours I've stood in front of a three-way mirror during fittings.) The good news is that over time this constant exposure to the reality of how you measure creates more of an acceptance about the surface imperfections, especially when you have a longer career. Bottom line, the fit model who isn't able to talk about their body measurements objectively, without shame or being otherwise triggered that a measurement is off would never survive this business. An attitude of body positivity and self-confidence inclusive of physical flaws is a must.

I've done this so long-my first contract fit modeling began in 1996 and lasted ten consecutive years-that I don't even know how to feel shame over my measurements. They just are what they are: 34½" bust, 27½" waist, 38½" hip, 22" thigh. All of these measurements are at the fullest point (wherever you can get the biggest measurement) with exception to the waist measurement which is done at the natural waist, or the smallest point. I have a slight waist shape, but I am not curvy or hourglass. My height is 5'7½". My head circumference is 22". And I have many other measurements all over my body from my arm muscle to inseam and, yes, even my ankle, that are the same or within range of a quarter inch of the fit form (or mannequin) that I've worked alongside to achieve the perfect fit in mass production of clothing garments.

These are just facts. Statistics. These numbers are not at all a measure of self-worth or perfection in being. Most of my measurements (but not all) match up to the perfectly-proportioned fit form of the company I've worked for. That's all.

Lastly, one big misconception about fit modeling is that because we have to maintain our body measurements within a certain tolerance this means we are constantly dieting. However it is the exact opposite. If you talk to any fit model who has been working for any length of time you will most likely find that not one of them diet. We generally eat healthy foods, but we don't "go on diets." There is absolutely no way I would have had any longevity in this career if I did try to diet or to severely restrict food intake for days on end. Starvation does not fall under my "perfect" category by a long shot.

Why should you care about this, and what do my experiences with fit modeling and weight consistency have to do with you? The average adult weight gain over the age of thirty is estimated to be 0.6 to 1.7 pounds per year.[2] This can be problematic, not just for trying to squeeze into last year's jeans, but because weight gain from early to middle adulthood (approximately from ages 20 to 55) has been linked to an increased risk for several chronic diseases, and a decreased likelihood for healthy aging.[3] While I am not a doctor or

2 Andra Picincu, CN, CPT, "Average Increase of Weight in Adults," *livestrong. com,* 2019, https://www.livestrong.com/article/142567-average-increase-weight-adults/.
3 Jama Network, "Weight gain from early to middle adulthood linked to increased risk of major chronic diseases, death," *eurekalert.org,* July 18. 2017,

nutritionist, what I can provide through physical proof is that it's possible to eat well and even enjoy treats as you age without becoming a part of the above statistics.

In reading about my experiences I hope this helps to generate within you an appreciation about how your body craves, consumes, and digests food as well as moves and breathes in its own natural way that it was designed to do. At the very least I hope you learn to redefine the word perfect and maybe even start thinking "Hell yeah, I'm perfect!" towards a society that keeps telling us otherwise.

Because you are perfect. Who you are is important and wonderful exactly as you are now. And I thank you for even picking up this book to read what I'm about to share in order to help you solidify your own perfect version of you!

Chapter 2 - **Any Size**

In a more enlightened society, every body type and size would be normal, and everyone would feel empowered not just to accept but to celebrate themselves however they naturally are, wherever they fall along the measuring tape or land on the scale. But in this day and age it can be hard to find appreciation amidst all the "you need to look like this or that" noise out there. You'll need to block that out to find YOUR perfect, natural size.

Simply put, your size is the frame you were born to grow into. It's genetics mixed with calorie intake combined with how many calories you burn. Your perfect size is not one in which you are starving or when you stuff yourself on a regular basis with unhealthy foods. The size that is perfect for you is the size you are when you feel well-nourished and have ample energy to get through your day.

Finding that just-right size is about knowing where you best land on the scale. What is your weight when you're eating the proper amount of nutrients for your body? What are your measurements when you feel healthy and energetic and can enjoy physical activity?

> The secret is to NOT aspire to being a specific size. It's the opposite! What are those numbers when you feel great? *That's* your natural size.

Simply step on a scale or get out the measuring tape and use either of these as tools of measurement. A consistent routine check-in will help discover your range, or tolerance, of a few pounds higher or lower on the scale or slightly bigger or smaller along the measuring tape. But do NOT use these tools as a marker of self worth. They are weights and measurements. Facts. Numbers that assist you to determine your size.

I usually check in once a week first thing in the morning and I prefer using a scale over a measuring tape. This is because it's hard to measure yourself properly when you're not standing up straight, it takes more time to get accurate measurements than simply stepping on a scale, and you can cheat by pulling a measuring tape tighter or looser. The scale doesn't cheat. But remember the "muscle weighs more than fat" principle and that sometimes weighing more can be a good thing if your body is going from fat to muscle or is underweight. Most importantly, it's about keeping a healthy and mindful approach to what you put IN your body on a daily basis that determines your health rather than the scale or your measurements. It's not-nor ever was-nor ever should be-about the smallest number possible.

Knowing your natural size SHOULD equate to freedom from worrying about what size you think you should be or what size anyone else is. YOUR SIZE AND SHAPE IS AS INDIVIDUAL AS YOU ARE. So why is it then that it's hard to appreciate ourselves in all our wonderful shapes and sizes without that judgement that can come from all angles within us and outside of us?

I blame insane societal pressures. We can't change society's unrealistic standards single-handedly. But there are many ways to help combat the negative self-talk we all do to ourselves at one time or another.

For example, a good friend of mine named London who I met through modeling years ago told me that she had found a photo of herself as a little girl with a big smile and all the confidence of the world shining through. She said she put that photo of herself on her refrigerator at home and looked at it whenever she felt those negative thoughts about herself come up. She asked herself if she would say those negative thoughts to that beautiful, spirited, carefree child. Of course she wouldn't, and neither would we. We wouldn't even talk to our friends the way we do through our thoughts when we beat ourselves up about how imperfect we think we look.

Or have you ever looked back at a photo from the past as a younger adult and thought, "I looked incredible!" but then remembered how insecure you were about some physical aspect of yourself during that period of your life? Wouldn't it be great if we could all come to a place of appreciation in the present?

So choose your words and your thoughts carefully. Be kind or at the very least realistic when stepping on the scale or looking in the mirror rather than let the wildly exaggerated negative thoughts and ideas about yourself take charge. Find a beautiful, confident photo that you love of yourself to remember who you truly are. Place that photo somewhere you will see it every day to begin to realize that you ARE in fact perfect in ANY body shape and in ANY size.

Chapter 3 - **Any Age**

If you're my age you've probably seen several body types go in and out of style throughout your lifetime-proof of how subjective it is to judge body shapes and sizes at any age or stage of life you're in. Rail-thin, heroin-chic Kate Moss was the aspiration in the 1990s as was Twiggy back in the 1960s. More recently the curves of the Kardashians are "in style," similar to the 1950s when Marilyn Monroe's hourglass figure was coveted.

Over the course of my decades-long modeling career I have had direct comparisons of my body to what's currently "desirable" while working alongside a form that changed. My first contract for fit modeling was in 1996. Back then, at the same measurements that I am now, I was a size 8/Medium. Now, decades later, again AT THE SAME MEASUREMENTS I'm a size 6/Small. My inanimate "body twin" of 1996 changed shape and size within a span of twenty years.

I remember that once in the late 90s I was called into an intense meeting with a VP and several managers while they were discussing my body as being too small for them. The result was a decision to rename my size as a 6 instead of an 8, thereby extending my contract for many more years at the same measurements. This sizing change over time is called "vanity sizing" and was created by marketers to reflect the collective growing waistlines of our society. (I didn't care what size they wanted to call me, I was just happy to extend my contract and cash more checks.)

Seeing this process firsthand solidified the knowledge within me that there is no "perfect" body type, which made it easy to begin to accept myself as I was in my twenties as well as now, decades later. I value that knowledge more and more as I go through changes as I age.

Some of those changes I've experienced with age are the inevitable slower metabolism and digestion changes. My body is also softer in plenty of places than it used to be. The good news is that I actually feel better in my 50s than I did in my 20s and early 30s when I required more damage control for all of my less-than-healthy choices. Yes, better! And yes, it's an attainable goal to aspire to feel at least as good as we did in our youth as we age, which is all a part of finding our perfect.

Years ago I attended a college football game, and during the halftime show a man-a former gymnast-lightly jogged up the stairs to the stage to receive an award. I believe he was around 90 years old. I remember being shocked looking at how agile he seemed while effortlessly bounding up those stairs. Of course, he had gray hair and plenty of wrinkles on his smiling face. But his energy, his agility, and his ability to move his body so gracefully at that age was unlike any other older person I had seen. It made me wonder why that ability to move throughout life as we grow older isn't the norm, rather than the exception. That man will forever be my inspiration for what's possible.

More inspiration comes not only from other models and fit models that I've worked alongside throughout the years, but also from some of my close friends outside of the fashion world that eat and live very similarly to the way I do. I'm far from the only one who's achieved the level of consistency I've experienced. I'm not a unicorn and these wellness methods I describe in detail in the following chapters can work for anyone with a desire to make them work.

My friends and mentors all have in common that they feel good, they look healthy, and they've maintained their natural size as they've aged. That's who I like to follow-the people who are older than me with as much energy as they had in their 20s—or more! I mean, anyone can look and feel good when they are young without much effort. So show me some energetic, vibrant 50-somethings or older who don't live in Hollywood and don't have a glam squad, fitness trainer, and a personal chef at their disposal and I'm going to be open to listening to what they have to say.

So, at ANY AGE, rather than ignoring your body's warning signals-leading to a major overhaul-start to notice the things you may be doing that aren't working or those things you could improve upon. Let the things you discover direct you to altering course or fine-tuning as necessary. Because thinking you already have all the answers provides no room for growth.

> Instead, continuing to be teachable, flexible, and open to learning new ways of being is the secret to remaining agelessly perfect at ANY AGE throughout decades of a well-lived life.

Chapter 4 - **Whatever I Want**

I eat whatever I want, whenever I want. I have for decades while maintaining my measurements. It's not only possible for others to eat similarly without significant weight fluctuation but I believe it's also the most natural way for our bodies to eat regardless of metabolism, size or age. And guess what? Nothing you enjoy eating is off limits. Moreover, you can and should tailor your food to your tastes in whatever way brings you the most pleasure.

I discovered how to eat this way despite having to maintain my measurements under contract, by learning how to eat what makes me feel good. For example, clean, whole foods with the occasional sugary treat makes me feel good. I don't calorie-count or portion-control because neither makes me feel good. The only trick is learning exactly what makes you feel good-which foods give you the most innate pleasure.

And yes, that's what I'VE learned. But can YOU really, truly eat whatever YOU want and feel good and have energy, while maintaining consistency at the right weight for YOUR body? Yes!

Let me explain it this way. Everybody eats and nearly everybody has sex, or else we would literally die out as a species. Both are natural, innate parts of us, and our bodies inherently know what to do. I don't know why we as a society have so much guilt and stress about two of the things that were designed to give us pleasure in an effort to sustain life. Pleasure drives our choices. And pleasure drives our hunger for more.

So I like to get as much pleasure as I can from the way that I eat. It isn't nearly as intense as the sexual kind of pleasure, of course, but the way I eat feels good-especially when I treat myself to something creamy and sugary every week. But most importantly (even without the sugar high from a weekly treat) I feel so properly satiated and well-nourished with the whole foods I eat on a daily basis that it feels good in its own right, albeit a different kind of good-a satisfied good in answer to hunger signals that are naturally designed to alert me to eat. A feeling of being well-nourished and satiated during your meal and after you've eaten is naturally designed to let you know you're fueling your body with what it needs to thrive.

For example, red watermelon isn't my favorite but yellow watermelon-which I only eat a few times a year when it is in season-is absolutely delicious. (Shout-out to my good friend Tim for all the summertime Farmers Market drop-offs which include said yellow watermelons.) Whenever I eat it on a warm summer day, it tastes ridiculously scrumptious. As good as cake (and I LOVE cake). While I'm savoring every bite of several cups' worth, I inevitably say between bites to whoever is around me (or to my dog if no one else is), "OMG, how good is this watermelon?!" I repeat this several times in case I wasn't heard the first time, because it's that good-all while my dog looks up at me questioningly like, "Huh? It's just a yellow watermelon."

Speaking of dogs, think of how they react when they get real salmon freshly cooked from the oven, or scrambled eggs (if they're like my dog, in which case she does what we call "the Happy Egg Dance"). That's how good real food makes them feel and that's how much we should be enjoying our food. Well, maybe we don't need a happy dance per se but you get the point-they LOVE real, whole food, and we do too, at our core. Dog dances aside, no doubt it's the natural fruit sugar that my body and my taste buds love in the above example. But even if you hate yellow watermelon, there are plenty of clean foods that can give you that feeling of pleasure.

To begin finding those foods, pay attention to everything you consume WITHOUT judgment. Make a list of all the foods you eat. Do this for several weeks straight. Next to each food item, add a second column titled "feeling." (Sample chart in appendix.) Start to notice how different foods make you feel, regardless of what you think your favorites are.

In the beginning, it may take some time to feel within. Be patient with the process and keep trying. Focus on your energy level (both after your meal as well as throughout the day), your digestion, and your mood (anxiety, fatigue, etc). Try to pinpoint the exact feeling you experience when you've eaten that food. Be specific. For example: content, satisfied, fulfilled, or even proud of yourself for making choices that serve your nutritional goals. Or you might choose the feeling of being unsatisfied or wanting more food a short while later, gassy, a "food coma" fatigue, or even a feeling of being sick. Pick any feelings that seem close. Make sure absolutely everything you eat and drink goes on the list.

Eventually, you should begin to notice the foods that your body digests well, that give you a feeling of being full without being overstuffed, and that keep you from feeling like you need more food an hour or so later-and the foods that do the exact opposite. Start crossing the latter off your list one by one while you increase consumption of the former. Continue editing your list as you read the next chapter.

Over the years, I had subconsciously created my own mental list while paying attention in this way to all different types of foods and the effect they had on my mood, my energy, and my measurements. This has created an overall awareness of what works for my body and what doesn't. For example, despite the fact that I love sugar, I am now clear that the sugary treats I eat occasionally wouldn't taste as sweet if it was on the regular menu. Because I've over-consumed sugar too many times to count, I know it's simply not as special nor as tasty when I eat it daily.

My body feels good when it knows it's going to get the clean foods it needs to run efficiently, and it rewards me by making my food experiences full of pleasure. My brain now knows that, too, and is aligned with my body. And that is what creates harmony around my food choices.

That's the secret to eating whatever you want without significant weight fluctuation from your favorite fit model. (Yes, me.) To be able to eat this way, your brain and your body have to want the same thing-which is to get the most innate pleasure from what you consume.

Even if I'm not even close to being your favorite at this moment, and you're rolling your eyes at me right now, thinking that you don't have a fast metabolism so this won't work for you-it's not about how fast or slow your metabolism is. It's about properly nourishing your body on a consistent basis and your body rewarding you for your efforts by feeling good and having energy. Or, if you're thinking you're too old to make changes-you're absolutely not, because your world can change in an instant with new information at any age-if you let yourself be open to learning something new. Or, if you're thinking that you won't look like this person or that person-you won't. You'll look like your best *you*. Or, if you're thinking you won't be a certain size you have in mind that you're aiming for-you might be right. But you'll be feeling good at whatever size and shape that's natural for you. Or, if you think that you just can't do this for any other reason-you're wrong. Yes the fuck you can.

You know what is true, deep down. You can feel it. If you can tune into that feeling, you can reframe your thoughts around what you innately want to eat versus what you used to think you wanted to eat which will help you to believe it is possible. This mindset shift is what's most important in making the upcoming information work for you.

Think right now of a thought that is true for you. Anything you already genuinely feel, from "I'm open to changing the way that I eat" to "I can eat as many healthy foods as I want when I'm hungry." Write that thought near the top of your food list. Every time you add another food item, repeat that thought to yourself. This will help retrain your brain to remember that eating clean, whole foods is going to feel good at a cellular level. Your brain will then eventually catch up to what your body already instinctively knows, which can be summed up like this: *clean food is the amazing partner you're happily and contently committed to on a daily basis. Warm chocolate cake is a hot lover on the weekends. And a salty pretzel is a one night stand in a bathroom stall while on holiday.* Delicious.

Be open to the belief that your food consumption should never bring you guilt and should only bring you the natural pleasure it was designed for. If it's not, you're doing it wrong. (Your sex life too, but that's another book.)

And if you're confused about what exactly "clean" or "whole" foods are at this point, don't worry. Simply turn the page. It's time to eat.

Chapter 5 - **Nutrition**

As I've said, you are perfect exactly as you are. You have a choice-as in all things-to read the following chapters and change nothing. You are still perfect, of course. What is important, though, is that you not only believe you are perfect, but that in general, most days, you FEEL your best. Of course, we all have days where we feel anything but perfect, but the goal is for those days to be the exception rather than the rule. Proper nutrition can help.

Unfortunately, chances are high that you don't feel your best, or that you have improvements to make in regard to your eating habits. A Mayo Clinic study derived from the U.S. National Health and Nutrition Survey found that 97% of American adults do not have healthy lifestyle habits. The four basic indicators of health that were assessed include: a healthy diet, moderate exercise, not smoking, and keeping body fat in a healthy range.[4] Only 38% of Americans are eating healthy! And only 3% have all four daily healthy lifestyle habits nailed down?! Based on those numbers, many of us have some things to learn.

I've separated the nutrition portion of the book into the following sections:

HOW DO YOU WANT TO FEEL?
CLEAN, WHOLE FOODS
PROCESSED FOODS
THE FOUR STEPS OF UN-PROCESSING

---

4 Robert Preidt, "Less Than 3 Percent of Americans Live a Healthy Lifestyle," HealthDay News, March 22, 2016, https://www.medicinenet.com/script/main/art.asp?articlekey=194453.

PORTIONS
WHAT I EAT
HOW I EAT

HOW DO YOU WANT TO FEEL?

So how exactly do you want to feel? This is the MOST IMPORTANT QUESTION you can ask yourself, because the answer to this question inevitably drives what you want to eat. It's time to look over the list you've made and make a decision.

Do you want to feel good, or do you want to feel tired, depressed, and heavy? Do you want to feel constantly hungry by eating empty calories from processed foods, or do you want to feel satiated? Do you want to feel pleasure when you eat at every meal, or do you want to feel guilt or stress? Your answers are important, because you will probably NEVER make the right food choices for your body if you don't first focus on how you want to feel.

When you get to a point where you decide you don't want to feel bloated, sapped of energy, or undernourished on a continuous basis, you will start eating what supports that goal. You will use your list to begin eating based on the way it makes you feel. I mean, at either a conscious or subconscious level, who doesn't want to feel well-nourished?

This became my goal as I developed an awareness of what different foods did to my body while working as a fit model. I could feel, as well as measure, what was happening with different foods I ate, which led to creating lifestyle choices around nutrition and changed how I eat to this day. However that's not why I continue to follow a healthy diet and lifestyle.

Recently someone asked me what my book is about. I replied that it is about the lifestyle choices I've developed around my experiences as a fit model that have kept my measurements exactly the same. She replied, "Wow, that sounds exhausting," with a bit of judgement in her voice. Now, I had just run three miles right before speaking with her, and I felt great. I'm proud of the fact that I can keep up with my son while I'm in my fifties. I thought about replying, "Not really, but this conversation is exhausting." However I kept it to, "Not really."

This conversation has come to me in many forms over the years. It is exhausting, because it implies I'm going against nature and denying what my body needs in order to be a specific size. But it's the exact opposite! I attribute my long career as a model and a fit model—at least in part-to my desire to educate myself around wellness and nutrition. And ironically-for someone working in a technically superficial industry—this career has led me to feel okay in my own skin.

Would I have been so curious about what different foods did to me if I hadn't been measured regularly? Or would I have kept eating the highly processed foods I thought were healthy at the time? Would I have wanted to learn to meditate if I hadn't had the stress of day-long fittings while trotting the globe completely jet-lagged? Would I have developed an objective appreciation for my own measurements and size had I not seen it from a pragmatic standpoint for so long? Or would I have aspired unsuccessfully to be like someone else's body type? Would I have fallen in love with my workouts? I don't know, but I'm grateful that this path led me to where I am today.

So no, it's not exhausting to be who you are. It's exhausting trying to be like someone you're not and never will be. It's exhausting carrying around excess body weight for your frame. It's exhausting to treat your body poorly and live your days trying to keep up when your body isn't properly fueled. This, not modeling, is why I choose to make nutrition and lifestyle choices that make me feel good and inevitably look my best to this day.

At our core, what feels good is being well-nourished by giving our bodies foods that fuel it properly. That will never be untrue. And especially as you age, your body will let you know if you're doing a good job or if you're fucking it up. Listen to it.

Here's what to listen for: What are you hungry for, exactly? If you've just eaten, are you hungry for food? Or is it really about craving some other kind of energy like entertainment or stimulation due to boredom? Or do you need sunlight, a bath, a hug, or are you tired, do you need sleep, or water? Remember to check in with your environment as well as your body. Are you stressed out? What is causing the stress? What can you do to proactively ease the stress? At least pause and ask yourself the question before you grab the unhealthy snack or give in to some other unhealthy habit. And remind yourself that unhealthy habits will only add to the stress. Check in. Listen. Take a few breaths.

A good trick is to ask yourself if you're hungry for something healthy. If veggies, a piece of fruit, whole grains, or a healthy protein source sounds delicious, then you're hungry. If asparagus sounds yummy, then you're starving. (Sorry asparagus, but you are not my favorite vegetable.) If a healthy option doesn't sound good but the cookie or potato chips do, then you're probably not really hungry.

A similar version of this trick is to always eat something healthy before the junk. You want some ice cream? Okay, but eat an apple or some nuts first. You want some chips? Eat some crunchy raw veggies with hummus or steamed edamame with a bit of sea salt beforehand. It's more calories if you still eat the treat, but adding in the healthy snack first is a good way to start craving the food your body actually needs.

If you still overindulge on the unhealthy treats, go easy on yourself. Try again next time. Have compassion for your journey. No one gets it right every time. Shoot for getting it right most times or even more often than not. Then fine-tune. Keep going. Onwards. Upwards. It's a process! What matters most are your DAILY HABITS, not what you do on occasion.

So, make a decision once and for all about how you want to feel. Write it down at the top of your list. Ann Wigmore, a holistic health advocate of the 20th century, said, "The food you eat can be either the safest and most powerful form of medicine or slowest form of poison." Only you can decide if you're going to let your food be your medicine or your poison.

CLEAN, WHOLE FOODS

Foods that are considered "clean" or "whole" are the foods that make up the majority of my diet. By eating clean, whole foods at least 80% of the time, this allows for treats in moderation up to 20% of the time. This enables me to eat rich or high-calorie foods in small doses. It makes what I eat a lifestyle plan-not a depletion plan. And this is how I maintain my measurements, increase my immunity, and fuel my body for maximum energy while still getting the most pleasure from my food, making both my brain and my body aligned in regard to what I eat.

What are clean, whole foods exactly? The healthiest version of a food will always be its most natural version, unadulterated with food manufacturers' added salt, sugar, artificial sweeteners, artificial flavors, high fructose corn syrup, and preservatives. This is true no matter what the marketing on many packaged food items claim. Therefore eating clean, whole foods could be described as eating closer to the farm and farther from the food factory. Essentially, eating more of these nourishing foods and less highly processed, depleting foods is the goal when "eating clean."

Clean foods include fruit, vegetables, legumes, nuts, seeds, whole grains, dairy, eggs, and lean meats. However my body prefers a whole-food plant-based (WFPB) approach for the majority of my meals. This means that in addition to minimizing overly-processed foods, I also minimize eggs and dairy and eliminate meat.

Should you eat meat, eggs, or dairy on a daily basis? That's up to you, of course! That's a question you should genuinely be asking yourself. No one can make these decisions for you. You shouldn't take my word for anything. I'm just a guide, and these are my experiences that work for me. Pay attention to how you feel while continuing to write it down on your list. Get additional information by seeking out reputable websites and books about nutrition. Don't rely on one person or something you happen upon in an article you read that justifies something that you wish were true. Focus on what works for you.

In addition, it's not necessary to label your diet as "clean," "whole," "plant-based," or any other label. These are just descriptive words of the foods I consume and I will use them interchangeably. This is not "a diet." There are no official rules to follow aside from educating yourself about nutrition and becoming aware of how the foods you consume make you feel.

PROCESSED FOODS

It's not necessary to eliminate all processed foods in order to "eat clean." (Even chopping foods technically makes them processed.) But it is important to keep an awareness of the ratio of the clean versus the processed foods you eat and to become knowledgeable about the quality of the processed foods you do incorporate into your diet.

While some additives are needed to preserve the shelf life of packaged foods, some can be dangerous. This is why reading the ingredient labels of all processed foods is important. For example, some of the top dangerous food additives to avoid are: sodium nitrates, sulfites, trans fats, Monosodium Glutamate (MSG), and artificial colors.[5] These and several other dangerous additives found in many highly processed foods can cause chronic diseases, ranging from high blood pressure to heart disease and even cancer.[6] Rather than try to learn a long list of additives to avoid or to minimize, it's much easier to skip those overly-processed food items altogether. Especially if you don't

5 "5 Food Additives You Should Avoid," *Cleveland Clinic Health Essentials,* December 29, 2020, https://health.clevelandclinic.org/5-food-additives-you-should-avoid/.
6 Ibid.

recognize the additives listed on the packaged food ingredient label. None of the "foods" with these additives fuel your body or fight disease.

To begin finding the least-processed foods, start looking at the ingredient labels carefully. Focus on buying items with ingredients you recognize. In general, the fewer ingredients (five or less) the better.[7] For some specific packaged-food items to add to your grocery list, I recommend Dr. McDougall's approved canned and packaged food list which you can find at drmcdougall.com, a reputable plant-based, low-fat website.[8] Print out the list and take it with you grocery shopping to help you get started. If you don't have the list on hand, check the sugar, oil, and salt contents as percentages of calories on the labels. If any of those numbers are high, or if they are one of the first five ingredients listed, they are not your best choices, either.

Now that you have an idea of which packaged foods to avoid, get out your food list again. Create an additional column. Beside each food and feeling already listed, mark a "C" for clean, "P" for processed, and "HP" for highly processed (meaning foods with ingredient labels that have dangerous additives). (See appendix for an example chart.) Notice if there is a pattern between the foods that feel good in your body and those that don't. Either way, continue to tune into your feelings. Notice the effects that the clean, minimally-processed foods and the

---

7 Dan Buettner, "Blue Zones Diet: Food Secrets of the World's Longest-Lived People," https://www.bluezones.com/2020/07/blue-zones-diet-food-secrets-of-the-worlds-longest-lived-people/.
8 John McDougall, "Acceptable Canned and Packaged Foods," *drmcdougall. com,* https://www.drmcdougall.com/articles/free-mcdougall-program/can-ned-packaged-foods/.

overly-processed foods have on what you crave and how you feel.

Begin to separate your meals so that your highly processed foods are consumed at a different time in order to get an even more accurate read on how these foods are making you feel. Even better, you could start your day with clean, whole foods so that you can feel the effect before the overly-processed foods weigh-in.

While eating mainly whole foods, you may still have cravings for overly-processed foods. (Although you might start to notice that your tastes begin to change pretty quickly.) I still love sugary, baked treats and probably always will, but I now wonder how I ever liked some of the other junk foods that I used to eat. They now taste disgusting! Most physical cravings ease into non-existence, because when your body is well-nourished, it's not screaming for junk. The mental cravings due to boredom, stress, or habit are the ones that stay-until suddenly they don't anymore. That's okay. Just occasionally give in to those cravings while focusing on looking forward to and fully enjoying your weekly treat. The better you feel, the more your mind will understand what's happening, the more you will want to increase your good feelings, and the more your wants and habits will shift to craving clean foods.

For any mental craving that lingers on too long, you can try a technique called "Urge Surfing." It can be a helpful way to learn to avoid acting on those behaviors you'd like to reduce or to stop altogether. Find out more about this technique from Dartmouth-Hitchcock Health system.[9]

9   "Urge Surfing," *Dartmouth-Hitchcock Health,* https://www.dartmouth-hitchcock.org/sites/default/files/2021-03/urge-surfing.pdf.

The important thing to remember is that you most likely WILL crave processed, surgery, or fatty "foods" if you don't eat a clean, varied diet containing the proper nutrients and number of calories for your body. For example, just because kale is a densely nutritious whole food does NOT mean you want to eat it all day long and nothing else. Balanced, clean eating incorporates the proper portions of proteins, carbohydrates, healthy fats, vitamins, minerals, fiber, and water. All of these macronutrients are needed to help us maximize our energy, fight disease, and feel our best.

Another thing to keep in mind is that despite being clear that you want to eat clean, peer pressure is real. Be aware of this and know it will take some adjusting in social situations. Have a plan in mind before your social events and stick to it, or else use those moments for your treats. I generally do the latter. Have responses prepared so that when someone says, "Oh, you HAVE to eat a piece of this cake, I made it just for you," you can say something as simple as, "Thank you, but I'm not hungry yet, and I would love to enjoy it when I am hungry a bit later," or something similar that works for you.

Whether socializing or hibernating, whatever you choose, this is YOUR BODY and these are YOUR nutrition choices. It's always your decision what to eat and when to eat. A proper mindset rather than mindless eating is key.

If any of this sounds like it won't be easy, know that it may not be. Especially in the beginning and especially if you're transitioning away from eating a diet high in overly-processed foods. Most diets and supplement manufacturers out there say, "Follow our easy plan!" But eating clean takes focus and determination in the beginning, because we live in an overindulgent, packaged, drive-through, fast-food culture. Don't go into this thinking it's going to be easy. Go into it thinking it's going to be hard. Get ready to fight for your body, your mind, and your health. Only after your habits form into a routine that works for you will you find that it really isn't hard. In fact, it's truly enjoyable to discover all the scrumptious new whole-food options available to you. And then you too will be eating whatever you want and loving how it feels.

THE FIVE STEPS OF UN-PROCESSING

To begin un-processing your current diet and incorporating more whole foods, you need to leave the past behind. Your food choices from decades ago up to yesterday DO NOT MATTER.

As a matter of fact, I grew up on Captain Crunch, Doritos, and Little Debbie's snack cakes. I have heard the phrase, "What doesn't kill me better fucking run," and I love to apply this to nutrition. Whatever you put in your body is in the past. You know better now, so what hasn't yet killed you better fucking run!

For me that's the bad effects of the processed junk of my youth and the drugs and excess alcohol of my younger adulthood. While growing up I didn't like meat and I still don't. But I also didn't like vegetables (unless you count French fries as a vegetable, which of course I did in my teens). We ate a lot of canned vegetables back then, and I'm sure those canned veggies didn't have very clean ingredient labels. There also weren't many legume choices in my household. The menu was very meat-

and-potatoes, like a lot of American families' kitchens were in the 70s and 80s. I only learned to like vegetables and a variety of legumes and other plant foods as an adult in my twenties. And if my teenaged junk food and forever sweet-toothed body can learn to like vegetables and stop eating so many processed foods, so can yours! Trust me on this-Little Debbie's a bitch. So concentrate on the here and now with these five steps...

1. *Remove the junk.* Get rid of all of the processed food in the house. Yes, all of it! If it is not in the house, then you can't eat it (at least not conveniently). If there is a plate of cookies in front of me, I am going to eat some-if not several. So cookies don't live at my house, unless I'm planning on enjoying them as a treat. Make it so that you have to go out of your way to get the unhealthy treats you mindlessly snack on. If loved ones who live in your house complain, don't try to force change on them. Just communicate your "why" for this change and ask for their support by keeping their junk food in a cabinet out of sight. Focus on YOUR best health. Lead by example so that even if your candy-loving partner is not on board initially with your clean eating, they may see your results and eventually join in. Also, you're the boss of yourself AND your kids. If the kids aren't on board, too bad. You're the one buying the groceries and preparing the meals. Hopefully one day they will appreciate that you are giving them the priceless gift of proper nutrition. Regardless they will still get plenty of junk food at the grandparents' and friends' houses or from their candy-loving dad. And if they eat healthy foods

regularly they will be in better moods. From toddler to teenager, anything that helps with attitude is a good thing!

2. *Plan your meals.* Meal planning doesn't have to be a huge, time-consuming task. Simply look ahead at the week to come. Think about whether you have any special events coming up in the week where you would like to treat yourself. Allow for one or two treats throughout the week to look forward to. Plan to stay on track the rest of the week. Also think about the time of day when you struggle the most. Ensure that you have healthy options available to you for that time of day. If you struggle with preparing a healthy dinner, consider freezing some of your healthy favorites so you always have an option on hand that you can quickly heat up. If you live by yourself, freezing individual portions is a great way to be effective and efficient with your time and money. Being on-the-go working, parenting, and traveling are also times to consider what healthy snacks you have on hand. If it's difficult for you to remember to eat clean foods while at work, running the kids around, or traveling, then pack your snacks and meals ahead of time. The most important thing is to always make sure you have healthy, quick and easy options available while eliminating the unhealthy foods from your daily routine.

3. *Grocery shop.* Once you have your weekly meal plan in place for the coming week, it's time to hit the grocery store to shop for the needed clean-eating ingredients. Stick to the perimeter of the grocery store as much as possible for your veggies, fruits, and proteins. For produce, fresh is

best and frozen is fine. Canned foods can be an easy way to get your whole foods in, and it requires less planning since there is a greater shelf-life than fresh, but with any canned foods make sure you check the label. I eat canned beans all the time, as well as canned corn, tomato paste, and pureed squash, but most of my veggies are usually fresh or frozen. After your trip around the perimeter, head into the aisles strategically and only to get specific items like the canned foods, oats, rice, quinoa, nuts, nut butters, vinegars, oils, and condiments. Again, watch the labels on all packaged items for extra salt, sugars, and oils. I know checking labels can be time consuming if it's not something you've done before. An "approved" packaged food list like Dr. McDougall's can be helpful in the beginning of un-processing your diet. However, once you get used to knowing what works, you'll only need to check a new item occasionally and you'll have no problem zipping in and out of the grocery store with a full cart of clean foods. If you're not a fan of grocery stores, consider online ordering for pickup or delivery. This is also a good idea if you think you'd be tempted to buy other things that you don't need. We all know how to shop online after living through the pandemic of 2020 but as a reminder, Amazon Fresh, Thrive Market, and Instacart are great options. Instacart delivers groceries from local stores including Whole Foods, Target, Costco, and Petco in less than 2 hours! This is a good option for those who struggle with planning ahead. Lastly, there are also many prepared, whole-food delivery options which equate to having your own personal chef at home. They are more expensive, but if you don't like to cook and you can afford it, take advantage of clean, whole meals delivered to your doorstep.

4. *Meal prep.* Another valuable habit that can help you transition to eating clean as well as save time during a busy week is doing a weekly or bi-weekly meal prep. Meal prepping on the weekend works best for people who work long hours during the busy work week, but find whatever time works for you. Try to make it a routine. My approach to meal prep is pretty simple. I tend to make meals and eat the same thing for several days. I most often do a beans & whole grain dish, switching out the legumes and the grain the next time I make it. To this base I add in different veggies and eat it for several days. I chop things as I go throughout the week, and I also buy bags of shredded veggies to throw into meals, onto salads, into smoothies, or to eat alone. I sometimes prepare mason-jar salads. The basic recipe is to put the dressing and the heaviest ingredients at the bottom and the lightest leafy greens on the top to keep them fresh for several days. Make these to taste with whatever your favorite salad ingredients are. I also sometimes eat overnight oats which is a very simple version of a meal prep and will keep in the refrigerator in an airtight container for up to five days.

5. *Eat mindfully.* Eating mindfully is my favorite step. It not only makes you think about the quality nutrition you are feeding yourself, but food truly tastes better if you slow down enough to appreciate what's on your plate.

In contrast, if you don't think about what you're eating and instead just shovel food in while you're doing other things, you can't feel what's going on inside your body to appreciate whether it's even that good or not. And you'll probably eat more than your body needs. By creating awareness around your food choices, this step will help you discover how to eat in a balanced way. This will allow you to avoid the extremes of eating so little that your metabolism goes into starvation mode (which, if done repetitively, results in not being able to eat much of anything without gaining weight), or of eating so much that your digestive system wreaks havoc on your body while piling on the body fat. So be mindful when eating. Try to eat without distractions-not on your phone, not in the car, not multitasking, etc. It's okay if this step doesn't happen every single time you eat, as it's hard in our busy lives not to multitask on occasion. Still, for the most part, try not to rush your meals and to be as present as possible when eating. Beginning to regularly eat mindfully will help you to read your body and to truly enjoy what you consume.

PORTIONS

Just like tuning in to how you feel helps you eat the right TYPE of food, eating the proper AMOUNT of food also requires that we listen to our bodies. We start out our lives doing this instinctively as we were all made with natural inner cues to tell us when we are hungry and when we are full, just like all the other wild animals in nature as well as children (who can be mistaken for wild animals if they are in the right mood and environment, as any parent knows.)

If you have kids that have gone through a growth spurt or have had a really active day I'm sure you've seen this in action. I have witnessed my son eat about twice as much food than he normally eats and not nearly as much the next. Thoughts of how much he's "supposed to eat" never enter his brain. His body knows. And his hunger signals are spot on.

Just like your body knows how to heal a wound or keep your heart beating without you thinking about it, your body naturally knows how much and what kinds of food you need. If you are eating a variety of clean, whole foods with all the macronutrients your body requires, you can stop thinking judgemental thoughts about how much you're supposed to eat. Eating the right amount without judgment becomes easy to do because that is what our bodies were naturally designed to do.

Problems can arise when you think, "I should only be eating this much." No. You should listen to your body and feed it the clean, whole foods it craves when it's hungry and until it feels satisfied. But because a lot of us don't listen to our bodies, both under-eating and overeating occur, potentially making us even more judgmental about ourselves.

Even if we are not judging the quantity of what we eat, portion problems may also be due to many other factors. Some of those factors include stress eating, the effects of certain drugs, or eating disorders, all of which require consulting a professional.

Portion control issues can also arise from a lack of quality sleep. Ghrelin, known as the hunger hormone, is affected by sleep.[10] This means that if you're sleep deprived you will feel hungrier than if you regularly get a full night of sleep.[11] Therefore sleep is not something to habitually cut back on if you want to curb overeating, or if you value your overall health. Use a bedtime reminder on your phone, a white noise machine or whatever you need to get a proper night of sleep.

Another important factor that many are either unaware of or simply choose to ignore is that portion control is exacerbated by the consumption of high-fat animal products as well as oils, sugar, and other refined carbohydrates that are in highly-processed foods.[12] This is why it's so important to reduce those foods. I highly recommend the book *The Pleasure Trap: Mastering the Force that Undermines Health & Happiness by Douglas J. Lisle and Alan Goldhamer* which covers this and more in depth.

In essence, you don't need to restrict your portion size to remain at a healthy weight. It is the CONTENT of what you eat that keeps you from over-consumption.[13] When we eat the foods that disrupt our natural, internal cues of when to eat and when to stop, we over-consume and lose track of what our bodies really need and thrive on.[14]

---

10 Malcolm K. Robinson, MD, FACS & Laura Andromalos, MS, RD, LDN, CDE, "Sleep More to Eat Less: How Sleep Affects the 'Hunger Hormone,'" *brighamhealthhub.org,* https://brighamhealthhub.org/controlling-the-hunger-hormone/.
11 Ibid.
12 Douglas J. Lisle and Alan Goldhamer, *The Pleasure Trap: Mastering the Force that Undermines Health & Happiness*, Summertown, TN Healthy Living Publications, 2003, 74 - 82.
13 Ibid.
14 Ibid.

Food manufacturers use additives to not only preserve the life of their foods but also to keep us eating what they are selling with added sugars and fat which can be disruptive to our bodies. Those companies want your money. But you pay not only a financial cost-you pay at the cost of your health which is priceless. They profit while we get fat and sick. Fuck them. Stop the junk food addiction. Instead give yourself the respect you deserve by giving your body the proper amount of clean foods it needs to thrive, thereby eliminating the need for portion control altogether.

In addition to content, it may also be important to look at the CALORIC DENSITY of the foods you consume. This is especially true if you feel like you are eating well overall but continue to have more than your normal weight fluctuation. For example, dried foods are high in caloric density and are a concentrated form of sugar. This means that if you eat a tiny pack of raisins (or any dried fruit) you won't feel as full if you eat the same amount of calories as when eating grapes (or the actual fruit.) This is because the water content in the grapes naturally fills you up more. The result is feeling like you've eaten more after you've eaten grapes than if you'd had the raisins-even when eating the same amount of calories. So if you're not hungry but you are craving something to chew on, pick a small portion of dried fruit. If you're hungry, pick the fruit.

Nuts and seeds, both of which I eat daily, are another example of foods high in caloric density. There is no need to eliminate these foods. However, an awareness of the portion size with any foods high in caloric density is the exception to the rule of dismissing portion control while eating whole foods.

While using your food list, pay close attention to both the highly processed and the high-calorie dense foods you consume. Note the effect they have on your level of satiation. If you are eating meat or dairy regularly, pay attention to the effect of the high fat animal products as well. That list may be all you need to rely on to learn to actively listen to your internal cues. However, if you feel like you need additional help to find that middle ground, using an app on your phone could be another good resource.

There are calorie counting apps, apps providing nutritional education, and apps to track your weight. Some apps also calculate your macronutrients as percentages of your calories when you log your daily foods. This is especially convenient if you are transitioning to eating more plant foods and want to make sure you're getting enough protein. And even if you consider yourself a nutrition expert, it's also a quick, easy way to check in if you want to know exactly how much sugar or salt you're consuming in a day or if you want to increase your fiber. Knowing the exact percentages of how much protein, carbs, fat, sugar, fiber, sodium, or cholesterol you consume by simply logging your food for a few minutes a day can be incredibly helpful information, whether you're just learning or fine-tuning. Logging your food is also a way to be accountable, organized, and focused.

Which app is best for you is based on your needs and your knowledge around nutrition. Use an app in addition to your food list as a tool to help you discover how much you need to eat for your body type as you become in tune to listening to your body's own hunger signals. While you're finding that "just right" place within, try several apps to see what suits you best (view suggested options on paidtobeperfect.com). Many of them are either free or cost just a few dollars a month. Consider making that phone you carry around with you all day work for your health rather than against it (hello too much social media and click bait articles-of which I am definitely guilty.)

Once you are able to listen to your body to know how much to eat, the rest gets a whole lot easier and a lot more fun! Just like with your grocery shopping list, once you know what foods work, you won't need your food list or the apps anymore. It feels good to get to the place where you don't have to worry about portions or calorie-counting and you can just enjoy what's on your plate while eating your delicious whole foods until you feel satisfied.

Eating clean, whole foods is the direct route to cutting out the internal junk food chatter and truly discovering what nourishes you, what satiates you, and ultimately what makes you feel good. So let's talk about all these amazing options, starting with protein.

WHAT I EAT

protein sources

If you choose not to eat a whole-food plant-based diet, you can still eat clean while getting protein from eggs, dairy, and lean meat. Since I rarely eat animal foods I often get asked where I get my protein. Eating a variety of clean, whole-plant foods allows for plenty of protein in my diet. I consume densely nutritious, fiber-rich protein by eating nuts, seeds, legumes, oats, and quinoa to name just a few.

For a little extra protein (and because it satisfies my sweet tooth) I also like incorporating a vegan pea protein powder, usually in my smoothie. Keep in mind any "meal replacement" powder in a can is NOT replacing an actual meal. Nothing processed can truly take the place of what nature made. My vegan pea protein powder is a supplement that I use to get a little extra protein, and its sweet flavor tastes good in my smoothie and in my oats, which makes it feel like dessert. However, first and foremost I rely on all the natural plant proteins grown from the earth for proper nutrition. Having said that, my two favorite protein supplements are Vega One and LIV body. Stevia and monk fruit are used as sweeteners in a lot of protein powders, which you want to limit overall, so read the ingredient labels carefully and go easy with anything processed.

You can buy quality protein powders for around $50 or less on Amazon or at any Whole Foods or most other grocery stores. Be wary of "miracle" powders that cost significantly more than that and the people trying to sell them to you. And remember that protein powders are an extra-a supplement-that CAN BE added to an already healthy diet, NOT a requirement, NOR a shortcut for proper nutrition.

I DON'T rely on fake meats like veggie dogs or veggie burgers. Yes, they are fun for cookouts. But I don't recommend relying on them for your daily protein intake. Fake meats are processed foods, not whole foods. Eat them occasionally if you like them, but WHOLE FOOD plant protein is best.

If you're interested in eating plant-based protein but you think it would be hard to get enough, it's important to realize that people with a healthy and normal caloric intake in developed societies are generally NOT protein deficient, including vegans. In fact, what's more common in developed societies are health issues such as heart disease and certain cancers which arise from too much protein from animals and dairy.[15] Check out *The China Study* by T. Colin Campbell and Thomas M. Campbell if you want to delve into this further. It's a great read!

In addition, the website bluezones.com lists the diets of the people that live the longest in the world. To save you a click, yes you guessed it-the longest living populations eat whole-plant foods for 95% of their diet and eat animal foods only in minimal amounts (twice a week or less).[16]

Maybe you don't care about living a long life. Maybe longevity isn't your goal. That's fine and is certainly your choice. But for however long you are on this planet it's the quality of your life that is important. Being young and malnourished doesn't feel good. And it is the quickest way to *feeling* old and unhealthy while you are still young AND *becoming* old and more unhealthy with a long list of issues, medications, restrictions, etc-if you're lucky enough to make it into old age. Feel good while you're here for as long as you're here, right?! Seems like a no-brainer to me.

To be clear, I'm not saying you have to give up animal consumption altogether. If you can't imagine your life without

15   T. Colin Campbell & Thomas M. Campbell, *The China Study*, Dallas, TX, BenBella Books, Inc., 2016, 54-58, 107-111.

16   Dan Buettner, "Blue Zones Diet: Food Secrets of the World's Longest-Lived People," *bluezones.com*, *https://www.bluezones.com/2020/07/blue-zones-diet-food-secrets-of-the-worlds-longest-lived-people/*.

animal food, but you would like less saturated fat and more fiber, there are ways to enjoy meat without making it the main part of your diet. For example, consider making animal foods more of a treat that you only enjoy occasionally, like once or twice a week. That way you can have something to look forward to. Another option is to flavor your plant-based foods with meat stock while transitioning away from eating meat as the main staple in your diet. For example, you could add a low-sodium meat stock to a whole grain like quinoa, rice, or farro. I personally don't do this because I don't like those flavors, but those who do say they really enjoy the taste and smell of animal food cooking. This makes it possible for them to transition away from eating large amounts of meat. At the very least, if you do opt to eat meat or dairy regularly, you might consider adding extra fiber-rich whole-plant foods to those meals. Plant foods are naturally low in saturated fat and high in fiber, whereas animal foods are high in saturated fat and lack fiber and are therefore harder to digest. That's one reason why WFPB eating naturally requires less portion control and calorie counting-you get more fiber and get full easier.

Another additional benefit of eating whole-plant foods is that it's better for the planet, because it reduces your carbon footprint. So it's a win-win-win when it comes to being good for you, good for your savings account (plants are less expensive than meat), good for the planet, and it's obviously better for the animals as well.

However much meat you do decide to eat, consider purchasing it in the best way for the animals as well as for your health. I personally believe that the intense fear experienced by factory-farmed animals leads to excess hormone production. These hormones are then ingested by the humans eating the meat, and potentially disrupts our own hormones. This is debatable, and it is just my gut feeling (I have no research to back it up). But knowing how factory-farmed animals are treated, it's just something I've always felt to be true. Regardless, you might opt to purchase free-range, organic meat and dairy products whenever possible, because it's the kind thing to do.

carbs

Unless a doctor has determined you have an allergy to certain foods or any other medical condition, then you need to rethink any diet that eliminates or drastically reduces carbs. Carbs are not the enemy. On the contrary, our bodies draw fuel and energy from carbs. They are a necessary part of a healthy diet. Not eating carbs would be like trying to drive your car without fuel. You won't get far. The same thing will happen to your body and your energy level if you try to eliminate carb intake-you are going to run out of fuel and fall flat on your face. And that's not a good look.

Carbs themselves are not bad. It is the TYPE of carbs you are eating that cause issues. The carbs to eliminate are the processed, simple, refined carbs such as cookies, crackers, microwave popcorn, overly-processed breads, and yes, even the granola bars that are marketed as "healthy." These foods spike your blood sugar and your energy, then send you crashing down a short time later.

Many of these factory foods have been stripped of their whole-grain outer shell and then "enriched" to try to give the now lifeless, nutritionless grain something that resembles nutrition. And that's not all. The food manufacturers then take the white, powdery, enriched flour and add in "fillers" to help drive the cost down.[17] And this could potentially impact your health. To top it off, the factory foods might have added sweeteners, colors, or preservatives. THIS is what is fucking up your gut and causing you to overeat-NOT complex carbs!

Complex carbs are carbs that burn slowly in your system and provide a steady source of fuel and energy for your body. Think of complex carbs as something that you could get right from a farmer such as oats, beans, brown rice, quinoa, potatoes, and even some sprouted grain breads and whole grain breads that don't have added fillers, dough conditioners, and preservatives.

I tend to eat more beans, oats, quinoa, farro, barley and rice than pasta. But if you like pasta, there are plenty of healthy options to choose from. Check the packaged food list from Dr. McDougall for several specific brands.

fruits & vegetables

Eat them. Every day. Eat some at every meal. Eat some as snacks. Put them in your smoothies. Have some in baggies ready to grab and go. Just do what your parents always said and EAT YOUR FRUIT & VEGGIES! Fresh is best, frozen is good, and canned with a clean ingredient label are nice to always have on hand. There are so many to choose from and so many ways to prepare and eat them. Steamed, raw, sauteed, blanched, blended in your smoothie, in a soup, in a box, with a fox-wait, wrong

---

17   Tony Wagner, "How wood got in our food, then out of it, then back into it again," *marketplace.org,* Nov 1, 2017, https://www.marketplace.org/2017/11/01/how-wood-got-our-food-then-out-it-then-back-it-again/.

book. If you're thinking "But I don't like vegetables," well, you're not four years old (despite just reading a sentence inspired by Dr. Seuss), so get over your veggie aversion. Find some that work (like tomatoes, corn or potatoes), and find a way to incorporate them into your daily diet. Include different colors and plenty of leafy greens. The more varied the better, and you're guaranteed not to be bored.

If you can afford organic produce, great! But the most important thing is eating your fruits and vegetables, period. If the organic options aren't in your budget, just wash your conventional produce thoroughly with fruit wash or plain water. Also check to see which foods land on the Environmental Working Group's "Dirty Dozen" list on ewg.org.[18] These are the fruits and veggies that have the highest pesticide levels. If you can afford some organic options, buy organic for whatever you eat from this list. Also check out the "Clean 15" for produce which contains the least amount of pesticides.[19] If you want to save a little money and buy conventional, these are good choices. The lists change over time, so check them once a year.

<u>fats</u>

There are healthy fats, and there are bad fats. I eat healthy, unsaturated fats like raw, unsalted nuts, nut butters, seeds, flaxseed oil, olive oil and avocado. I eat these DAILY but in MODERATION. Here is one place to pay attention to portion size, because these foods lack fiber and are high in caloric density.

---

18 "EWG's 2021 Shopper's Guide to Pesticides in Produce," *ewg.org,* https://www.ewg.org/foodnews/dirty-dozen.php.
19 "EWG's 2021 Shopper's Guide to Pesticides in Produce," ewg.org, https://www.ewg.org/foodnews/clean-fifteen.php.

Therefore your body's signals may not register the calories until well after you over-eat them. Fats have high caloric density, so you don't want to overdo even the healthy fats on a daily basis. But know that these healthy fats can be an important addition to your daily nutritional needs to help keep your body running efficiently.

Saturated fats are found in foods like butter, coconut oil, bacon, red meat, and cheese. Eating too much saturated fat can affect your blood cholesterol levels. Consumption of saturated fats should be limited.[20]

Even more dangerous than saturated fats are trans fats. These fats come from partially hydrogenated vegetable oils such as deep-fried fast foods, doughnuts, margarine, vegetable shortening, and many manufactured baked goods. Trans fats not only raise your bad cholesterol and lower your good cholesterol, but they also have been shown to cause inflammation in the body that can lead to disease.[21] No thank you.

<u>fiber</u>

A properly functioning digestive system is important for a healthy body. Therefore plenty of fiber in your diet is key. As you learned in the protein section, if you are eating a whole-plant food diet, it's naturally filled with fiber. However, you might feel that your daily fiber intake could use a boost. One option I like which ensures good digestion naturally, easily, and

20   "The Skinny on Fats," *heart.org,* Nov 11, 2020, https://www.heart.org/en/health-topics/cholesterol/prevention-and-treatment-of-high-cholesterol-hyperlipidemia/the-skinny-on-fats.

21   Joe Leech, "What Are Trans Fats, and Are They Bad for You?," *healthline.com,* July 30, 2019, https://www.healthline.com/nutrition/why-trans-fats-are-bad.

inexpensively is to grind up a tablespoon or two of flax seeds in a coffee grinder. Most days I sprinkle them on my salad, on my oatmeal, or in my smoothie. Voila. Cheap, easy, and your tummy will thank you. You can buy them in a pre-ground powder, but I buy flax seeds whole and grind them fresh daily to preserve the nutrients. I'd suggest trying it both ways for a couple of weeks at least to see what works best for you. The coffee grinder method is super easy, though-and that's coming from someone who likes to keep things simple in the kitchen.

A word of caution about smoothies. Even though I love them, and they are a quick and easy way for me to get a lot of great nutrition, they can lead to overconsumption. If you are prone to overeating, I recommend holding off on smoothies altogether. Wait until you know what and how much to eat to truly satisfy your body and you are eating a healthy amount of calories for your body on a regular basis. The reason is because drinking your blended food can be less filling and satiating than chewing food up. Blending food disrupts the fiber.[22] So the same amount of calories you drink from a blender may not get you feeling as full as the same amount of calories from eating solid foods. For someone who can read their own body well, a blender can be your favorite kitchen tool. For others, it can be more filling to forgo the blended up or liquid calories (such as juices) and instead chew up the solid foods.

There are many other fiber-rich options including legumes and whole grains that should already be on your radar as foods you may want to incorporate into your daily diet.

---

22 Tom Philpott, "We Don't Mean to Ruin Smoothies, But…," *motherjones. com,* March 16, 2016, https://www.motherjones.com/food/2016/03/are-smoothies-devil/.

Fruits and vegetables, which you should be eating every day, are filled with fiber too!

sugar

I love sugar. Not just fruit. I love table sugar, Stevia, monk fruit, agave, honey, maple syrup and molasses. I love them despite the fact that all sugars and sugar substitutes are addictive and I know that I feel better without an excess of it in my system. Sugars create a spike and then a drop in your blood sugar. When the drop occurs, you crave the sugar again, eat it again, and feel another drop-creating an addictive cycle. Therefore all sugars (besides fruit) are best saved as a weekly treat.

Fruit is the best and the healthiest option. Whole fruit (not fruit juice) has fiber that balances out the natural sugar and gets absorbed into your system at a slower pace without creating the sugar highs and lows.

Added sugars, however, need to be limited to less than 10% of your total calories per day.[23] It adds up pretty quickly. This is another good use for an app to track how much sugar you consume in a day if you have no idea.

So if you have a sweet tooth, eat your fruit, because that's your body telling you that you need healthy sugar. (This is assuming you're not diabetic or have some other underlying health issue.) If you've already eaten some fruit and that didn't cut it, try dark chocolate (85% cacao or higher) or use any of the above sweeteners sparingly.

And be careful of "studies" justifying your unhealthy habits. As much as I want to believe the "studies" on an internet

23   "Get the Facts: Added Sugars," *cdc.gov,* May 6, 2021, https://www.cdc.gov/nutrition/data-statistics/added-sugars.html.

search about the natural, zero-calorie options, there are no miracle sweeteners. For example, I mentioned using Stevia and monk fruit above, but an excess of either of them raises blood sugar levels, causing cravings just like table sugar does. They don't have any calories which makes you think it's a good choice, but then later you're craving more sugar. Search monk fruit and Stevia on a reputable website like NutritionFacts.org and you will uncover the unfortunate fact that just because they are calorie-free does not make them a free choice to make without consequence.[24] All nutritional choices have consequences-some good, some bad. Sweetening your food tastes good (and life without that sweetness is unimaginable to me), but keeping it to a minimum and being realistic with zero calorie natural sweeteners is key.

Don't use artificial sweeteners like Splenda, Sucralose, Aspartame, or Acesulfame Potassium. These are found in many yogurts, sports drinks, and other processed sweet foods and beverages. The artificial sweeteners may reduce the total sugar grams in your system, however, artificial sugars also increase cravings for more sugar.[25] And more importantly, anything artificial is going directly against a natural, unprocessed, whole food approach which is what I follow and encourage others to learn about, because I know how good it feels.

Last but not least, fruit juices, even 100% fruit juices, are sugar without the fiber. Limit juice. Drink lots of water. You can

---

24   Michael Greger, "Is Monk Fruit Sweetener Safe?," *nutritionfacts.org*, July 9th, 2018, Volume 42, https://nutritionfacts.org/video/is-monk-fruit-sweetener-safe/.
25   Stacy Malkan, "Aspartame is Tied to Weight Gain, Increased Appetite and Obesity," *usrtk.org*, May 31, 2020, https://usrtk.org/sweeteners/aspartame-weight-gain/.

flavor sparkling water with a splash of your favorite 100% juice to have a taste of it without as much sugar. I also occasionally like mixing a little juice with almond milk as a fun, sweet, "creamy" drink.

The most important thing to remember is that if you are eating an excess of added sugar, then you are not giving yourself the best chance against sugar cravings. You will want more, and you won't feel good overtaxing your body with sugar highs and lows. Stop the cycle. Eat fruit.

<u>alcohol</u>

Unless you drink hard liquor straight, your alcoholic drinks also contain sugar. Too much alcohol can affect so many things about your state of being. It can veer you off course from clean eating by derailing your food choices either late at night while drunk, or the next day while hungover. Believe me, I know. I've been there and done both many times.

It's funny to me now that I used to drink Bailey's during the holidays and Pina Coladas on vacation. Now, I'd rather not pour the empty, sugary calories down my throat when I could have a yummy dessert instead. And yes those are high-sugar and high-calorie examples. Beer, wine, and hard liquor (without mixers) don't have the sugar that mixed drinks have. But whichever way you drink it, alcohol is still very calorie-dense. There is a 9 minute Youtube video titled "Do you lose weight when you stop drinking?" made by Annie Grace that explains this better than I can. Watch it to become aware of what the calories in alcohol do in your body. (Spoiler alert: it's not good.) In essence, even straight alcohol without sugar mimics sugar in your body, alcohol is high in caloric density, and alcohol inhibits your digestion of food by holding off digesting actual food in order to rid your body of the alcohol.[26]

I highly recommend also checking out Annie Grace's book *This Naked Mind*. If you want to drink less or quit drinking altogether because you want to reduce the empty calories, or for any other reason (including a more serious issue with drinking), this book and her videos are a non-judgmental, educational and inspirational place to start.

Alcohol is such a huge part of our society. Becoming aware of how it's affecting your nutrition is key, especially as you age. If you truly want to be healthy and feel good, NOT drinking your calories in the form of alcohol (by keeping your alcohol consumption to a minimum or eliminating it altogether) is the best way to keep your mind and your body in the best place. Heavy consumption of alcohol will not only make you feel like shit, but it will also derail all your best health efforts if you let it. So don't.

Here is how I currently navigate alcohol consumption:

1. *I don't drink on an empty stomach.* I've discovered I can't drink on an empty stomach (as if I ever could). As I age that fact has hit home hard. I will black out, vomit, have horrible headaches the next morning, and it makes my workouts miserable rather than enjoyable. I don't know how or why I ever thought I could drink on an empty stomach. Even one glass of wine on an empty stomach doesn't sound good to me anymore because, I know where

---

26   Annie Grace, "Do you lose weight when you stop drinking?," *youtube. com,* Oct 12, 2020, https://www.youtube.com/watch?v=svjC54uAvFA.

that road leads, which is more drinking on an empty stomach due to being buzzed off of one glass of wine, and my body eventually rejecting what I've done to it in some form.

2. *I am more mindful of my approach to alcohol.* Alcohol homogenizes your experiences.[27] Therefore the sporting event, the concert, the cookout, the bar scene, a nice dinner at a restaurant, your vacations, holiday gatherings, or even your evenings at home will all tend to have the same type of underlying deadened feeling, making everything blend together especially when alcohol is used in excess.[28] That understanding resonated with me personally when I came to the realization that I didn't want all my experiences to feel the same way. So rather than just drinking because it's nice outside, it's raining, or it's a snowstorm; rather than drinking because it's Friday or Saturday (which was literally what I used to do for years and years); rather than drinking because I'm at a social event; or at a movie; or because I've had a hard day; or it's a really good day; or any other kind of day...I drink now only when I have a plan to drink. I'm very deliberate about when I drink, who I drink with, and how often. Right now for me that equals out to a few glasses of wine once or twice a month. Drinking mindlessly is no longer something I like to do.

---

27   "The Unconscious Mind and Alcohol Addiction: Liminal Point 7: Is alcohol vital to social life?," *thisnakedmind.com*, 2021, https://thisnakedmind. com/unconscious-mind-alcohol-addiction-liminal-point-7-alcohol-vital-social-life/.
28   Ibid.

3. *I do me without judgment of others.* Some of my friends definitely didn't like it when I stopped drinking as much as I used to. I don't blame them. They were my drinking buddies, and I'm the one who changed that dynamic. But I don't care about how others will feel if I'm not drinking. I don't put any pressure on myself to fit in by drinking, and I don't expect anyone to fit into my way of doing things, either. I used to love drinking often, too, so I get it. We are all on our own paths, and I respect everyone's own personal journey.

4. *There are no rules.* I can change my mind about these "rules" I've set for myself around alcohol (or any rules) anytime I want to. This is what works for me today. That may change tomorrow. I do what works with whatever new information I have available to me. I have some idea of how that will look in the future, but I know that I need to remain open to whatever happens. Life is tricky. As soon as you think you have all the answers, something comes up to show you that you have something to learn. So I remain the student, I remain flexible, and I remain open to new ways of being in regard to drinking alcohol and in all things.

HOW I EAT

Now that you know what I eat, and how important it is to unprocess your diet as well as put a little planning into it, I can share with you HOW I eat. Some of this is a recap of the information above. This is my own personal "perfect" way of eating to sum it all up for you. I follow this with a condensed list of what I eat by food category in the next chapter for a quick reference.

But first, for any of you who still think I'm at the same measurements just because of my metabolism-no, I absolutely gain weight when I eat an exorbitant amount of highly processed junk food, just like everyone else. More importantly, I also know how stuffing myself regularly with junk feels. Do I still eat too much junk every now and then? Yes. I probably always will, maybe because I occasionally need a reminder of how I don't want to feel, which inevitably drives me back to eating clean. That's probably why I still drink too much wine once in a while-to remember how that feels and to remind myself I'm not missing anything at the very least.

So now that we've cleared up the metabolism myth once and for all, here is exactly how I eat.

plant-based whole foods

I eat a varied diet centered around whole plant foods. I don't eat meat. I limit dairy, fish, processed foods, alcohol and sugar. There are no foods that are off limits. There are simply the foods that I like to eat and the foods that I don't. I have no hard, set rules for myself other than listening to my body and doing what works. It's truly as simple as that. And because I've been eating this way for years, I know exactly what foods make my body perform the way I want it to, which inevitably makes me feel good and keeps my body at its natural size.

intuitive eating

I tend to prefer meals where I sit down and feel satisfied rather than grazing all day. I don't intermittently fast (I don't even know the official rules for that). But I do have an awareness not only of WHAT food works for my body but also WHEN it works for my body to eat and when it doesn't, which seems to align with what little I know of intermittent fasting. I don't plan on researching it or following any official intermittent fasting rules anytime soon because I believe listening to my body is what's most important.

I don't portion control and I don't calorie count. I eat when I'm hungry until satiation. Some days I eat more than what's normal for me. Other days not as much. On the days that I'm more hungry, I'll add in more plant protein to curb snacking on surgery or processed foods.

"Intuitive" is how I would describe the way I eat. I have done this naturally for years, starting from when I discovered as a teenager that my body didn't like to digest meat. I eat intuitively by going with my body's clock instead of an actual clock or an event like a workout. There are those who wake up and eat breakfast first thing in the morning, have a set pre- and post-workout meal or snack, eat their lunch, afternoon snacks, and dinner in a specific way and time. Being scheduled and regimented can work for some, but that's just not what works for me. I don't eat in a scheduled way, because that goes against what I feel is right for my body which is paying attention to my internal cues.

For example, I don't care what time I eat breakfast. Sometimes I'm not hungry in the morning, so I wait to eat when I am hungry, which could be lunch time. I know breakfast is supposed to be the most important meal, but I'm not a morning person and I'm just not into it most of the time. However if I do wake up hungry, which happens sometimes, then I'll eat something.

As another example, I rarely eat prior to working out. I also usually need some time after I workout before feeling ready to eat. I am generally not hungry right after working out, so I don't see the point of force-feeding myself. I fuel my body properly on the preceding day so I know I can get through whatever the next day holds. However, if I am hungry before or after a workout, I'll definitely eat. This works well enough for me. I clearly haven't wilted into nonexistence without consuming packaged, "supercharged" pre- or post-workout bars or "special" processed sports drinks.

The exception to this was when I did several "Tough Mudders" (a half-marathon with obstacles every couple of miles) years ago. I didn't know how much extra fuel I'd need to get through, so I ate extra calories during training and prior to the races themselves even when I wasn't as hungry. (I didn't add special bars or drinks, by the way. I added more clean, whole-plant foods.) Marathon runners carb-load before races to help them get through. Same concept. So if you are an endurance athlete, a professional athlete, or if you're aspiring to Simone or Serena status, you may need to eat a bit more than just when you feel like it. Pushing yourself beyond normal daily fitness levels is a different ball game altogether, as are your nutritional requirements during any illness or other health issue.

So assuming I'm not trying to be a badass, dinner is my most scheduled meal within maybe an hour or so time frame, though it still varies from day to day and from summer to winter. I have one kid and I have flexibility during the day, so I realize that's easier than if you have a bigger household or a tight work schedule. However if having a schedule is what works for you, you should absolutely adhere to one. Those of you who are working with set time breaks for eating or cooking for a large family will indeed need to be more scheduled, which will add up to your perfect nutrition plan. But if you're not hungry and it's "time to eat," make sure you're still focusing on healthy foods first which may not be as appealing if you're truly not all that hungry at that moment. The most important thing is to make your meals work within your day-to-day rather than try to mimic anyone else's "time rules."

form habits

While I don't do schedules or rules, I do form habits. For example, I often drink a full glass of water first thing in the morning and before lunch and dinner. This makes it easier for me to remember to drink water, especially because I'm not into carrying around a water bottle all day long. Even during 60-minute hot yoga classes, I know I'm already hydrated, so I don't even bother bringing a bottle of water to class. I also always try my best to make a habit of getting eight hours or more of sleep. Healthy habits are what creates the cumulative effects of all of your ongoing healthy choices.

recipes

I generally don't follow recipes. When I cook, my meals are made to taste by using whatever seasonings and flavorings I feel like. (My favorites are in the next chapter.) If you are into recipes, though, I recommend drmcdougall.com or forksoverknives.

com for many options to choose from if you are following a plant-based diet.

vitamins and supplements

Vitamin supplements are something I do take. But, like any other manufactured product or powder, I believe they are more of a crutch-the lazy way of getting my vitamins and minerals. The best way to get nutrients is to get it from whole foods. Except Vitamin D-the optimum way to get this is by absorption through your skin from exposure to a small daily dose of direct sunlight. That said, I do occasionally take the following supplements: vitamin D, vitamin C, a multivitamin, vegan Omega 3, B-12, the vegan pea protein powder I mentioned earlier, and sometimes I'll add in a probiotic. Supplements are generally more expensive than getting your vitamins and minerals from whole-plant foods, but they can be a good addition to an already clean, varied diet.

fasting & cleanses

I have done fasting and cleanses over the years. These can be useful as a seasonal reset, to help detoxify if you have health issues that need to be addressed, for religious purposes, or any other number of reasons. I won't share my own experiences here because it's so much more important to have healthy daily habits rather than to use fasting or cleanses. These are NOT sustainable as a healthy diet, and you WILL go back to your previous weight eventually if you don't change the foundation of your nutrition. Rather than a restrict & overeat cycle, education and consistency are key.

hard to easy

Is "how I eat" easy? Yes, eventually, once you get used to it. Because when you're eating clean, whole foods for the majority of your diet, you won't feel hungry until your body alerts you that it's time to eat. And then you simply eat. I've been at the exact same measurements since my twenties, and I'm not walking around starving because I'm not filling up on processed junk that DOES make you endlessly hungry. An excess of junk gives you a stomach that becomes an undernourished, bottomless pit.

It's easy because it's a natural, intuitive approach to nutrition and because you know you're going to treat yourself at some point during the week with whatever it is that makes your mouth water. For me that's sugary treats.

But remember what I said at the beginning of this chapter- go into this thinking that it's going to be hard, because it honestly may be in the beginning. Any change of direction takes some effort and some time to digest-figuratively and literally in this case.

healthy foods first

My son has heard me say the phrase "healthy foods first" hundreds of times, maybe thousands. He would probably say a million. This is because when he asks to eat junk as a snack my answer is usually for him to have something healthy like a banana or some nuts first. Most often my answer is followed by a big eye roll directed towards me, generally accompanied by a huge sigh. He'll then sometimes decide to eat the healthy option followed by the junk, but occasionally, he opts out of the junk food snack altogether. Even with the attitude, I love it when he fills up on whole foods and then forgets about the processed junk he originally thought he wanted. Those are my small but significant "mom-wins"-and the reason why he usually asks his dad for the junk.

> In essence, eating healthy, clean, whole foods that I genuinely enjoy first and foremost when my body says it's time to eat is the secret to how I eat. This is what makes me feel and perform at my best.

So consider clean foods your fuel. And know that however you choose to fuel yourself creates a domino effect-clean eating feeds upon itself, as does eating junk. If you start off your day with a doughnut, it's a lot easier to get derailed and a lot harder to make healthy choices the rest of the day (not to mention the moody sugar highs and lows that come with that doughnut). That's why making it a point to get in all of your favorite healthy foods first every day is the best way to feel good both mentally and physically. When you start to notice the differences in the way you feel, how your skin looks, how your hair looks, how much energy you have, how you work out and you notice the positive effects on your state of mind, you might consider making "healthy foods first" a part of your perfect, too.

Chapter 6 - **My Perfect Foods**

The foods in this chapter are a sample of my most consistent daily favorites.

- Fruits
  - Fresh fruits like an apple, banana, or grapes
  - Various frozen fruits in my smoothie like pineapple, blueberries, and jackfruit (Appendix - Smoothie recipe)
- Vegetables
  - Raw veggies like leafy greens, carrots, beets, cilantro, cabbage, and seaweed (a sheet of Nori) in my salads, or several of these in my smoothies
  - Cooked veggies with my dinner including potatoes, tomatoes, squash, cauliflower, and many others in my protein and whole-grain bowl
- Carbs chosen from the following sources of whole grains:
  - Quinoa, farro, barley, or rice mixed with beans and veggies
  - Old-fashioned oats
  - Sweet potatoes or Yukon Gold potatoes
  - Ezekiel bread or Dave's Killer Bread
- Protein chosen from the following sources:
  - Various beans/legumes mixed with a whole grain
  - Tempeh or tofu
  - Flax seeds (freshly ground in a coffee grinder to preserve the nutrients), chia seeds and/or hemp seeds

- Raw and UNSALTED almonds, cashews, peanuts, pine nuts, and Brazil nuts
- Vegan pea protein powder such as Vega One or LIV body in my smoothie or my oatmeal
- Cheese (limited to one or two portions per week)
- Wild Alaskan salmon (limited to one or two portions per week)
- Healthy fats used *occasionally* (in addition to the tempeh, nuts, seeds and weekly portions of dairy and salmon above:
  - Flaxseed oil
  - Olive oil
  - Coconut oil
  - Avocado
  - Nut butter
- Apple cider vinegar
  - I drink a shot of this in the morning mixed with fresh lemon juice, ginger, and stevia. Use a straw! Neither the apple cider vinegar nor the lemon juice are good for the enamel on your teeth. (Appendix - Ginger lemon cider shot recipe)
- Beverages
  - Filtered water
  - Decaf green tea
  - Decaf coffee
  - Plant milk such as almond or oat (Appendix - Almond/ oat milk recipe)
  - Sparkling water (occasionally flavored with bitters, a few drops of Stevia, or a splash of 100% fruit juice)

- Sweeteners (used sparingly)
  - Stevia
  - Honey
  - Cacao powder
- Spices
  - Mrs. Dash, everything bagel seasoning, cumin, cinnamon, turmeric, cayenne, ginger, rosemary, sage, thyme, pepper, salt, nutritional yeast, and Bragg's Amino liquids
- Weekly treats
  - cheese
  - a surgery dessert
  - a few glasses of wine on occasion during the month

You may find a few things from what I've shared that work for you. Or you might find several. Or you might say, "Screw you-I want a doughnut." If the latter is the case, eat the doughnut. Then come back and read this again another day. Because every day is another chance to recreate yourself and every baby step forward edges you closer and closer towards feeling your best.

And remember, these are my perfect foods. However, the secret to finding YOUR perfect foods is to eat the whole foods that YOU enjoy cooked and seasoned the way that you like best in an effort to always get the most pleasure from what you consume.

In addition, if you are interested in getting even more valuable information, visit paidtobeferfect.com. There you can find links for reputable doctors and organizations who advocate for the consumption of clean, whole plant foods as the cornerstone of proper nutrition through YouTube videos, websites, and books.

Chapter 7 - **Fitness**

Fitness is important, but you CANNOT exercise your way out of a bad diet. Therefore before reading this chapter and thinking you are going to exercise your ass off to compensate for your poor nutritional choices please return to the previous chapters and reread. When you're ready to dial-in your nutrition, only then will you be ready to achieve your fitness and overall wellness goals.

Unless you have persistent health issues, moving your body should feel good. If it doesn't, that's probably a good indication that you either need to eat better or that you've been sedentary for too long already, or both. It's time to start moving and become amazed with yourself by what your body can do.

To begin, get clear on WHY you want to work out and decide what your fitness goals will be. Personally, I don't work out for an end goal. Enjoying the workouts by moving my body in a way that feels good throughout the years IS the goal. Enjoyment as well as the physical benefits like heart health and a strong, agile body are in and of themselves good reasons why I workout but there are many other good reasons to make daily fitness a habit. For example, I consider my workouts my healthy, high quality "me time." When I run, it's my alone time, my moving meditation, my time with my headphones and a good beat to pound the pavement. Ideas and thoughts pop into my head while I'm running that don't come through when

I'm trying to multitask. Going for a run is also what I do if I have an excess of bad or sad energy of any kind to burn off. The rhythmic pounding left to right clears my mind and centers me every time. And those reasons are just as important as the physical benefits I'm getting, if not more so.

Yoga is my community-my time in a space with like-minded individuals moving together in a group as one. It's my time to bond with others, decompress, and breathe as well as become stronger and more flexible. It's my time to feel the group energy created in the room. Yoga is also my sanity. I can walk into a yoga class feeling rushed or stressed. A few deep breaths in, and those subtle, tingly feelings I get when I'm pleasantly grounded in the safe environment of the present moment begin as if on cue. After nearly every class I leave feeling better than when I had arrived. It melts all the stress away (literally, in fact, because some of the classes I go to are really fucking hot).

Because of these benefits and more, I know how much I NEED my fitness routine. Knowing how much you need fitness for both your body and your overall state of wellbeing is often what drives the desire to make a habit out of fitness. If you believe that your body needs physical activity daily, you'll do it because you want to. I think that's the main reason we do anything-because we want to. And if we don't want to, it won't get done.

Don't worry if you don't get those endorphin highs right away. In fact, if you're brand new to making daily exercise your "thing," you most likely won't. You'll be sore, and at least initially your muscles will loudly protest. But if you start to pay attention to how good you feel AFTER each workout, or even DURING each workout if you're at the level, you'll begin to trust the process. So give it some time-at least several months-for your body to find it's rhythm.

Adding the thought "I get to workout," is a great mental trick. It helps when getting started as well as anytime you're not in the mood. Whenever I think "I *have* to go for a run" (which usually happens when it's freezing cold outside), I sometimes need to add the thought, "Well actually, I GET to run." I start thinking about all the people that can't do what my body can do for various reasons. I know there are many people who wish they could just throw on some shoes and take a jog but can't. And that there are people who may actually like winter (as crazy as they must be to like freezing temps). Though to be completely honest, even with that mental trick it's still sometimes tough to get into the spirit right when I walk out the door to a burst of arctic wind. But overall if I remember to feel appreciation for the fact that I GET to run, it changes the whole experience-once I warm up a bit.

But in any season of the year, don't run at all if you hate running! And don't do yoga if you hate "zen." Those are two of MY perfect workouts (with some barre, pilates and dance classes thrown in to mix things up).

> The secret to creating a daily fitness routine for yourself is to choose activities YOU enjoy. It has to be something you look forward to.

For example, I don't like weight-lifting, so I don't force myself to lift heavy weights. I like using my body weight for strength (like planks or handstands), and occasionally I will use very light weights with repetition. The most important thing is to pick what YOU like to do, or it simply won't get done. Throw on your headphones and dance. Learn a TikTok video. Chase your dog. Jump on your kids' trampoline with them. Go sledding, skiing, swimming, or play basketball or tennis. Walk. Go on a hike. Ride your bike. Being in nature inspires athleticism, especially on a beautiful day, so add as many outdoor activities as you like any time of year. You'll be continuously motivated and never bored. And make sure your workout changes over time to accommodate who you are, which is always evolving!

While you're dreaming up your game plan, the following are some tips to help you along the way.

1. *Rewards.* If you need some motivation to get started you could reward yourself. (At least initially, because as you go, fitness itself becomes the reward.) Don't make it a snack or a treat reward, but something that takes up your time during the day that isn't as productive as a thirty minute workout would be. For example, maybe you're on social media too much. Or you binge watch Netflix. Whatever those unproductive things are that take up too much of your day, don't let yourself do them until after you work out. It's a similar concept to "healthy foods first." In this case it's "physical activity first." And maybe you'll eventually feel so good after you work out that you'll forget about your Instagram feed and just enjoy extra time in the shower giving yourself "spa time." Take time out to indulge in whatever you like to do for frivolous fun. You worked for it.

2. *Combine fitness with fun.* Another way to motivate yourself is to combine physical activity with something you already enjoy. For example if you are on a stationary bike or a treadmill, watch your Hulu or Netflix show. Or if you're outside, listen to your favorite music station or your favorite podcast on your headphones. Or run with your dog. My dog is only four pounds and is too little to join me on a run (though she enjoys the wind in her fur during bike rides in her backpack.) But I see how happy other dog owners and their dogs are who run together, so that's always an option to make it fun, too. Or make it social with human companions, a time for you and your partner or your bff to do some physical activity together. The social aspect is also a good way to have it on the calendar for some accountability if you struggle with motivating yourself. Or if schedules don't allow for social time, get a text group together so that you can send pictures of yourselves and congratulate each other with hive-five and trophy emojis. Or use Zoom or Facetime to work out together simultaneously from a distance. Be creative to make it motivating and fun!

3. *Put your workout clothes on.* If you work from home or if you can wear casual clothes out and about during your day, put on your workout clothes first thing in the morning. If you automatically put on your workout clothes, you'll be ready to fit in your fitness at any time of the day.

4. *Take time out every day.* For those perpetually busy people (which is all of us) who tend to think, "I don't have time to work out," change your thought to: "I CAN take 30

minutes out for myself, because it's good for me and I'll be a better human to those around me." Find the best time of day that works for you, which might even be different every day. Or break it up into little, mini five- to ten-minute workouts a few times a day. Or you can even take a short walk after every meal. Worst case, just park as far away as possible from every errand you run in order to walk greater distances, and take the stairs everywhere you go. Bottom line, we can all come up with 30 minutes in our day to get some form of physical activity. Make a decision. Put it on the calendar. And do it.

5. *Stretch.* Remember to stretch. Flexibility COMBINED with strength is the strongest, most balanced combination. Develop one without the other, and you're bound to pull something or get hurt at some point. I was given this analogy a long time ago: *A bodybuilder's muscles can snap like a twig if they also don't focus on flexibility. But a yogi is flexible and strong like a tall tree and can be blown whichever way and still remain standing.* I love that thought. Though flexibility doesn't mean you have to do yoga or the splits or even touch your toes. It means you are working on gently lengthening and allowing for your muscles to relax without forcing them. As a matter of fact, the more you try to force them, the more locked up your body gets. Therefore think of stretching as more of a "letting go" rather than forcing anything. Some workouts combine both strength and flexibility such as certain forms of yoga, pilates, and barre classes. Know that yoga, pilates and barre classes are NOT for wimps. I don't care

how much weight you can lift, these types of classes will still challenge you. I taught hot yoga for a few years, and I loved when male athletes (who without a doubt had more muscles than me) would come to my class thinking it would be easy and struggled to stay in the room. They left afterward completely drained and shocked at how difficult the class was for them. You will work your muscles and get toned in those classes. But even if those kinds of classes aren't your thing, remember you still need to stretch. So train like a strong tree while also working on being flexible enough that those strong muscles, tendons and ligaments you've created can't be snapped.

6. *Check in with yourself.* Ask yourself questions during and after your workout. Get curious about your response to what you're doing, especially when it seems hard. For example, I use my workouts as a time to go within to see what I'm made of. What do I do when the workout gets a little tough? What happens when my heart rate goes up? Can I slow it down by controlling my breathing? Can I find a rhythm? What happens when it's hard to push though? How do I react? Ask yourself, "What happens when it's hard?" If the answer is, "I give up," well, ask yourself, "What can I do differently to make it work for me next time?" Remain curious WITHOUT JUDGMENT while you answer those questions for yourself. Notice how both the questions and answers change from day to day.

7. *Accept failure as a part of perfection.* It's not only okay to "fail" on any given day. It's also a perfect part of the process. I've tripped many times while running and

have even fallen down more than once. (Thankfully one of my biggest spills was in the winter when I had heavy running pants and gloves, so I only ended up with minor scrapes and bruises. Uneven sidewalks suck, especially when you're in your groove and not paying attention.) My "failures" also come from occasionally pushing myself too hard. I've had migraines from hot yoga when I've tried to do it while I wasn't properly hydrated (pro tip-don't ever try that.) And I've given myself minor injuries when I've overstretched. I look back and think that if I would have given up after these setbacks, then I wouldn't have either running or yoga now-two things that are currently very important in my life, which I can't imagine being without. Yes, you will have setbacks. But keep going. It will not only get easier but it will become your daily reset and a part of "your normal."

8. *Acknowledge when you need a break.* You'll have "off days." Maybe you're beginning to feel under the weather or you have other circumstances going on. If you're sick or injured, those are the times your body is telling you to rest. Take it easy and get extra sleep to give yourself time to heal. When you're feeling better, begin again.

9. *Set some goals* for ages 30, 40, 50, 60 and beyond. What is it that you want to be proud of that your body can do? Maybe you want to be able to do a set amount of burpees when you're 40; or hold a handstand or do the splits at 50; or run a 10k or even a marathon at 60-or something else entirely, like climb a mountain. Or the goal could be as simple as walking every single day at 70, 80 or 90,

and beyond. Whatever it is, find that goal that makes you proud to say, "Hell yeah, I can do that", at any age!

Just like nutrition is about eating what gives you the most innate pleasure, fitness is about joyously moving your body in whatever way feels the best to you. It's about having enough energy to get up a flight of stairs without feeling winded at any age. It's about movement. Because our bodies weren't designed to stay stagnant leading to atrophy. You WILL lose what you don't move.

The good news (or the bad news, if you repeatedly make less-than-healthy choices) is that any small change you make with your nutritional habits as well as your fitness routine will add up exponentially over time. So every daily workout you incorporate, even if it's only 10 or 15 minutes, is still worth it. BOTH the healthy AND the not healthy choices are ongoing and you see in the present moment what you've created for yourself. So keep your goals in mind and be proud of what your body can do along the way. And maybe at 90 years young you'll be the one effortlessly jogging up some steps, motivating others to know that it's possible.

Chapter 8 - **Skin Care**

In the same way that nutrition affects your fitness routine, if you think you're going to have great skin as you age without eating properly and being well-hydrated, you're sadly mistaken. To look your best at any age, proper nutrition and a healthy lifestyle are more important than any lotion or potion you put on your body or anything you inject. Not drinking enough water, eating too many highly processed foods, not getting enough sleep, smoking, drinking alcohol-all of these affect the human body's largest organ: your skin. Therefore use quality skin care products as a COMPLEMENT to what you cultivate from within to enhance all the good nutritional and fitness habits you create for yourself.

> The secret to amazing skin is that you always need to start on the inside. The surface-level products you use are just the icing on the cake of your perfect, personalized skin care regimen.

Skin care is highly individualized, because we all have unique sensitivities that should be shared with our dermatologists first and foremost. However, here I share my own personal routine, because my skin is a combination of dry/normal/oily/ sensitive, depending on the climate-representing many skin types. This makes me hopeful that I can be a multifaceted guide for skin care and that I'll be able to share at least something that you will resonate with. For context, my ethnicity is mixed-from Africa, Asia, and Europe to the Americas, nearly the entire world map is lit up on my DNA chart. In addition, I've done plenty of my own research through trying all of the latest and greatest products in the market based on recommendations from make-up artists and other models throughout the years. And although I can't replace your dermatologist, skin care regimens remain as individual as we are, I share what works for me in hopes you find something in this chapter that works for you.

Overall I follow a preventative, maintenance-based approach to skin care. This is much easier (and much less expensive) than trying to fix deeply wrinkled, sagging, or sun-damaged skin. I also gravitate towards natural products whenever possible, while keeping it simple. I don't want to buy products labeled "oily skin" and then travel to a different climate and need "sensitive" or "hydrating." Therefore, with the exception of a few products, most of the products I choose work year-round because I keep my skin care routine stripped down to the basics that work. The cleaner and easier the more perfect for me.

As a general rule I think it's important to have clean, well-moisturized skin before bedtime. At the very least, use sunscreen daily, and wash your face to get your make-up and/or sunscreen off and put on some moisturizer every night. An even better approach, especially as you age, would be to add in toner and serums. I'll dive into each of those categories deeper as well as add a few more throughout this chapter.

Note that most of the things I'll mention can generally be applied to your neck and your upper chest, too. You'll run out of your products quicker but your neck and chest will match your face.

Lastly, I pick and choose where to spend the most money on skin care. I don't recommend spending a lot on everything. Just because it costs more doesn't mean it works better. So choose a few things that you love and are unmatched elsewhere in the skin care industry, and then buy reasonably-priced or drugstore skin care products for the majority of it. I have links to all of my current favorites on paidtobeperfect.com. But remember this entire book is about finding YOUR perfect. There are plenty of skin care lines out there to try. Have fun experimenting to find what works best for you.

<u>cleanser</u>

A sonic cleanser, which is one of my current favorite skin care tools, is a battery-operated, vibrating cleansing brush that gently exfoliates your skin while cleansing. You can buy them at most stores that specialize in skin care.

In addition to exfoliation, another benefit of a sonic cleanser is that it primes your face for whatever serums or moisturizers you use to allow them to sink in for maximum absorption. If I'm going to spend money on serums and moisturizers, I like getting my money's worth (who doesn't right?) I use it once daily (usually at night) with a gentle cleanser to remove any make-up or sunscreen to have my skin properly primed for the other products.

I think of it as a more natural way to exfoliate rather than using a daily exfoliating face scrub, because using this tool means you use fewer products than if you were to add in a micro-exfoliant scrub (this also makes it more cost effective). Those scrubs aren't bad. They certainly work if you find the right scrub for your skin type. But it's another product with more chemicals you're adding to your regimen and I personally like to keep it to as few products as possible.

The liquid cleansers I currently use in conjunction with my sonic cleanser vary, but they are generally inexpensive. I have used plenty of expensive cleansers over the years, and I personally don't find any of them to be more effective just because they cost more. You can find clean, quality, dermatologist-approved options anywhere.

<u>toner</u>

After cleansing I use a toner. Depending on which one you choose, using a toner can help protect your skin from damage. I like witch hazel because it's a powerful antioxidant. I also occasionally use colloidal silver because of its antibacterial and antiseptic properties. I often use toner solo first thing in the morning before working out instead of a cleanser just to wake me up and make my face feel clean. There are plenty of toner options out there that are inexpensive and work well.

<u>vitamin C and hyaluronic serum</u>

We all know how good Vitamin C is to ingest and for those of you who are new to serums, it can work as a topical for your skin as well. It promotes collagen, diminishes fine lines, and evens the skin tone.[29] Another great topical is hyaluronic acid which helps your skin retain moisture, making your skin

---

29   Deanna Pai, "These vitamin C serums can brighten skin, reduce wrinkles and more," *cnn.com,* 2019, https://www.cnn.com/2019/10/15/cnn-underscored/vitamin-c-benefits-for-skin/index.html.

look smoother.[30] There are many Vitamin C and hyaluronic combinations in the market to choose from at all price levels. In several skin care lines, the hyaluronic acid and the Vitamin C are combined into one serum. Manufacturers also sometimes add in additional ingredients that are beneficial to the skin like retinol, squalane, Vitamin E and aloe. I use it twice daily before moisturizer and/or sunscreen.

<u>sunscreen</u>

It's common knowledge how damaging too much sun on your face is. But if you need a reminder, you should use sunscreen on your face daily. Use any decent broad-spectrum sunscreen that doesn't block your pores.

I've also made it a habit to wear a hat and sunglasses if I'm outside in the sun for any length of time. I wear a visor when I run, and if I'm biking or walking my dog I wear a hat. My hat rule generally applies anytime I'm in the sun for over a half hour. So consider getting your vitamin D from the sun on the rest of your body with whatever amount of sun protection that your skin needs while acting like a vampire with your face and neck. If your face becomes lighter than your body you can either use a self-tanner or blend in a little foundation to match your body.

Sunscreen is one area that I use a different product depending on the time of year or the climate. Mineral sunscreens can work well in high-humidity environments or if you have oily skin. I prefer the ones that are slightly more liquid-based rather than the creamy ones because they act similar to a primer, taking

---

30   Hana Ames, "11 benefits of hyaluronic acid for the face and body," *medicalnewstoday.com*, 2021, https://www.medicalnewstoday.com/articles/hyaluronic-acid-benefits.

away the shine while creating a matte finish. In drier climates and especially during the winter, I like to use a moisturizing/sunscreen combination to make my skin more dewy and less matte. Either a mineral or moisturizing/sunscreen are good options depending on your skin type.

retinol

Retinol, a Vitamin A derivative, is an absolute must in my skin care routine. It is an exfoliator, it increases cell turnover (creating smoother skin) and it stimulates collagen production.[31] It's also anti-aging and wrinkle-reducing, and regular use can diminish breakouts as it helps to regulate oily skin.[32]

If you are brand new to retinol, however, take it slowly. Use it up to once a week before gradually increasing to more often depending on your skin type. This is because retinol's exfoliating nature could make your skin extra sensitive or even peel slightly when you first start to use it. Because retinol brings newer skin cells to the surface, make sure you use a broad-spectrum sunscreen after applying to protect your fresh skin (though you should be using a proper sunscreen daily regardless).

Once your skin develops a tolerance to retinol it can be used daily depending on your skin type. I tend to use a retinol in the evenings only when I'm not in the sun, which is why I like it in a separate product rather than combined with my Vitamin C/hyaluronic serum, which I use twice daily.

---

31   Rohini Radhakrishnan, ENT, Head and Neck Surgeon, "What Does Retinol Do for the Skin?," *medicinenet.com*, 2021, https://www.medicinenet.com/what_does_retinol_do_for_the_skin/article.htm.
32   Ibid.

I have tried many retinol topicals, and they all have pros and cons. Some are liquid like a serum and some are cream-based. They also have different percentages of retinol. So you will have to experiment a bit to find the right one for your skin type.

moisturizer

The creme I currently use is where I spend the most money on my skin care regimen. I've used it since my late twenties. Even though it's ridiculously expensive, I can't seem to live without it, because I know how well it hydrates my skin and helps me to maintain a smooth complexion in any area that is prone to wrinkles. I don't know for sure if it's one of the main reasons my skin looks the way it does in my 50s, but I'm not willing to switch it up just in case. So I pay a ton for it (despite the fact I'd love to break my expensive creme habit.) The brand I use is on my website. I won't mention it here, because inexpensive facial moisturizers do work, and I'm sure you can find one that doesn't cost as much. Search for ones that are dermatologist-approved with a consistency that makes your skin feel properly hydrated in any climate.

Lastly, I don't use a separate moisturizer for my eye area. I like using one high-quality product that works well for the delicate eye area as well as my face and neck.

make-up

I use minimal makeup these days. I used to wear a ton for modeling jobs. I think I just got sick of it. I also don't like the mascara removal process which disturbs the delicate area around my eyes, so I only use it occasionally. I dabbled in different lash enhancers for a while before I decided I'm okay without spider lashes. (For now anyway.) So my normal daily routine is blending in a bit of liquid foundation, brushing on a little powder, filling in my brows, and throwing on some lip gloss.

If you wear make-up, don't forget to wash your make-up brushes regularly. I use shampoo to wash them and let them air dry overnight.

oils

Facial oils aren't always a part of my daily routine. But I mention them here because sometimes in the drier months I will use a few drops of oil prior to moisturizing. Using an oil at night for deep hydration can also be a nice daily or occasional addition depending on your skin type. I also use oil with an electric wand, as I will explain later. I have experimented with several different oils, and overall I like argan oil. You should experiment, too, to see which you like best.

routine

Despite all the information I just gave you, believe it or not this entire process starting from cleansing only takes me minutes. So to sum it, up my topical facial skin care routine applied in this order is:

Day
1. Toner
2. Vitamin C and hyaluronic serum
3. Moisturizer
4. Sunscreen
5. Light make-up

Night

6. Gentle cleanser with a sonic brush
7. Toner
8. Retinol
9. Vitamin C and hyaluronic serum
10. Moisturizer

body

For my body I use inexpensive, clean, gentle body washes, baby oil, and unscented baby lotion. I also love dry brushing my skin before showering or using a natural loofah in the shower with a gentle cleanser. Occasionally I'll use essential oils depending on my mood and the season. I've been experimenting with body retinols (at a lower percentage than the ones you use on your face) lately as well.

LED mask

In addition to topical skin care products, I also use an LED mask regularly. LED light started being used for skin care after NASA discovered that in addition to helping plants grow in space, it also helped heal wounds quicker.[33] LED light has also been discovered to have collagen-producing and acne treatment and prevention benefits, and the skin care industry caught on quickly.[34] Red light was found to be anti-aging and blue light helped to prevent acne. There are also yellow/amber and green lights for similar benefits.

---

33 Mark Ellwood, "The Facial That Came From Outer Space," *bloomberg. com,* 2018, https://www.bloomberg.com/news/articles/2018-04-24/lllt-therapy-masks-like-opera-celluma-use-leds-for-beauty-facial.
34 Ibid.

What I like most about using an LED mask is that these benefits can be realized without being invasive, especially as someone who is not particularly fond of needles. Seeing results takes regular use and possibly more frequent use in the beginning and then tapering off depending on your skin. But just like everything else, if you get it on your schedule you can get it done.

My mask automatically shuts off after fifteen minutes, and I only use it occasionally, up to a few times per week. However, how long and how often to use one depends on the brand of the LED mask you're using as well as your skin type.

For me, using an LED light mask is calming. In fact, I prefer to use it in the morning as a meditative moment. I simply make sure my face is clear of any product prior, and then I lie down with the mask on and relax. Afterwards I do my normal topical routine as described above.

The different mask models vary in price so you need to do some research to find an LED mask that's affordable but still works well. You can buy one that has several different light color options, or you can buy one with the light that targets your main concern. While shopping around, know that LED light masks can be worth the purchase price if you make a commitment to use it per the instructions provided rather than let it collect dust.

high frequency wand

Another non-invasive tool I use is a high frequency wand. If you get facials regularly, your esthetician has probably used this on your skin. These electric wands help reduce fine-lines, providing a toning effect on the skin, and can also help with acne.[35]

The one I use has a slight electric charge feeling (like a mini-shock) with an overactive, buzzing, fluorescent office-light noise. As annoying as that sounds, I personally don't mind it at all. I use it up to a few times per week for about two minutes at a time although usage depends on your skin type as well as the brand of the unit you purchase.

I most often rotate between using the high frequency wand and the LED mask. I find those two tools complement each other well for my skin.

The wand I use must be used with facial oil to make it glide over my face because the wand itself is glass. I like to use it with argan oil.

It's not expensive to buy one to use at home compared to getting a facial at a salon. The fact that you can buy a device, like a high frequency wand or an LED mask to use at home rather than at a salon, med spa, or doctor's office is brilliant in its convenience. I personally love having fewer appointments on my schedule while having both the high frequency wand and the LED mask as part of the "at home" maintenance mix.

<u>botox</u>

There are plenty of options for injectables and other med spa treatments depending on the results you're looking for. Botox is probably the injectable most of us are familiar with, and it is the only one that I have personally tried. For those unfamiliar,

---

35 Simone Sydel, "How Often Can You Use a High Frequency Machine?," *theskincareculture.com,* https://theskincareculture.com/how-often-can-you-use-a-high-frequency-machine/.

Botox is a neurotoxic protein that when injected can temporarily relax your facial muscles thereby preventing wrinkles.[36] There are many people, men and women alike, who love injectables like Botox. It definitely has its uses in a maintenance-based approach to skin care. But Botox and other injectables also have risks due to the invasive nature.

I haven't had any Botox injections for several years, though I did like the results of Botox back when I did it. What I didn't like was the pain and the expense. I haven't written it off completely for the future. However I prefer my regimen described above without Botox or any other injectables for now.

micro-needling

One more thing I'd like to mention is micro-needling. Currently there are several options to choose from: standard micro-needling, micro-needling with radio frequency (RF) and micro-needling with platelet-rich plasma (PRP) (otherwise known as the vampire facial). Though I can't give first-hand feedback because I haven't personally tried any of these options yet, I have seen the results, and they look promising.

I haven't tried it because one, it's expensive as hell (up to several thousand dollars for a three-treatment series) and two, because I assume it hurts. They do use a numbing cream, but after having used numbing creams for both electrolysis and waxing on my bikini area, I don't trust those numbing creams. In any case, once I'm prepared to drop some serious cash and am able to gear up the mental strength to try micro-needling

---

36   "Botox-Type Injectables Guide," *americanboardcosmeticsurgery.org, https://www.americanboardcosmeticsurgery.org/procedure-learning-center/ non-surgical/guide-botox-type-injectables/.*

despite my apprehension of anything involving needling my face, I MIGHT be into giving it a go.

Pain and fear factor aside, what I personally like about the concept of micro-needling as well as both the LED mask and high frequency wand that I use is that they all fall under a more natural approach than injectables. So for now, LED red light therapy and a high frequency wand are what I currently prefer in lieu of the expense, the time, and the stress of any injectables in my face (while I try to get brave enough to maybe try micro-needling).

silk pillowcases

Another skin care maintenance tip that is easy and relatively inexpensive-silk pillowcases. Silk maintains moisture in both your hair and your skin whereas cotton pulls the moisture out. It also helps to alleviate the deep crease marks from cotton on your face if you're a side sleeper. You can find silk pillowcases anywhere. I like 100% silk, but I try to buy the least expensive set I can find because they don't last as long as cotton pillowcases. (Use the delicate cycle and air dry for longevity. However you'll still end up replacing them at least once a year or so.) You spend around eight hours on your pillow each night. For that reason alone, it's worth it to me. But I also love that it feels silky soft on my skin.

summary

It takes a minute to sort out the best skin care for yourself especially with all the new options the skin care industry comes up with regularly. But to me it's worth it to continue to perfect your skin care routine by remaining open to new discoveries in the market.

Whatever you decide to try with any product, tool, or treatment, always make sure you do your research and confirm with your dermatologist. The side effects can be numerous. You want to be well-informed of any potential temporary or long-lasting issues for your skin.

My best overall skin care advice is to wear your sunscreen in the daytime, rest your head on a silk pillowcase at night, focus on a daily routine of topicals that work for your skin type, and consider some non-invasive options before you try any of the more invasive treatments while keeping in mind that a little goes a long way. The more natural you keep yourself looking, the less upkeep. Regardless, I hope that whatever you do on the surface of your skin makes you feel a little better, and a little lighter on the inside, so that you can share that light with others on your path to becoming your perfect.

Chapter 9 - **Wellness & Mindset**

If you hate the appearance of your skin, start with your nutrition. If you can't even imagine working out, start with your nutrition. If you lack the energy to smile at least a few times every day, start with your nutrition. Everything, including your mental health, is enhanced or diminished by your nutrition. Of course your mood and overall state of mind can also be affected by many other things including clinical depression, a chemical imbalance, traumatic events, and grief. However proper nutrition is important, even if you need more than that as determined by your physician or therapist.

What is also important in addition to nutrition-especially if depression, anxiety, or any other mental health issues are the norm rather than the exception for you-is to ask for help. It shows your strength to ask for help when needed. There is only so much we can do on our own, and acknowledging this is powerful as well as transformative. There will be times, though, when you have all the helpers in the world and you're still not okay. We all have our highs and lows, our sadness, loss, anger, hurt feelings, and our days where we think everything is too much. I've had many days when I didn't want to get out of bed, let alone put forth any effort in finding the days' perfect. It happens. And those feelings are important to experience, too. But if they become too much, seek help.

Help can come from doctors and therapists, of course. But it can also come from friends, strangers, animals, or an unexpected source, such as a line in a song that pops on just when we need to hear it. And from books, of course! I learned about an incredibly helpful mental health technique (which I highly recommend) called Eye Movement Desensitization and Reprocessing (EMDR) therapy from Francine Shipiro's book *EMDR*. I then explored the technique more deeply with my own therapist. It's a powerful technique I highly recommend. Another book that I loved is *Healing Back Pain: The Mind-Body Connection* by Dr. John Sarno. It explains how stress can cause pain in your body and describes how some pain can be healed without medication by tuning into what is causing you stress. It's truly amazing what the mind can do when you're given the tools that work for you.

So wherever your help comes from, know that helpers are everywhere if we remain open to receiving some help. "Look for the helpers" is one of my favorite quotes by Fred Rogers and is often the beginning of being able to work through difficult times. Once through, it feels good to pay back the help you've been given to others when you're able.

It's important to remember that we all need outside help at times. However, the remainder of this chapter focuses on what we can do individually to help achieve wellness through our own mindset. Wellness incorporates an overall bigger picture of health. Wellness includes nutrition at its base but also requires a positive mindset, positive relationships, and a conscious understanding of what truly makes you happy and helps you be your best you. All of these elements are interconnected.

Read on to see what I do to help keep myself centered, which is the foundation for all of the fitness and nutrition habits I've maintained throughout the years. This chapter may be the most important of this book, because cultivating a positive mindset will inevitably lead you directly to your perfect.

I have several favorite wellness and mindset habits that I've used throughout the years. I'll start out with the one that's simple, straightforward and more universal than words: I listen to music.

MUSIC

Music therapy is powerful. Though I've known, I didn't use it as an actual wellness habit until the pandemic of 2020. I needed more tools than ever before when I wasn't going anywhere during the stay-at-home order. I needed to NOT hear the evening news, which my husband listens to religiously. At that time, I couldn't take any more news conferences and endless speeches while being quarantined for weeks on end. (As a rule, I generally can't watch the news and be expected to be in a good mood. I can tolerate the news highlights at some point in the daytime. But especially in the evening, I can't sit and watch news anchors and politicians babble on and on without it affecting me negatively. Knowing what you are, and are not not capable of helps in all areas of your life.)

So during the pandemic, when both my husband and I were in the house with no place to go and the news was on, rather than let THAT be my background noise, I started to regularly put on my headphones while listening to my playlists. This created a better mood instantaneously in lieu of listening to the evening news drone on and on.

And music therapy is not just for avoiding the news. I've used it in traffic many times. I'm sure we all have. I've also used it when my husband was grumpy and trying to start an argument with me. It's taken me many years to get to this place, but I realize now that rather than engage in someone else's bad mood and turn it into a big thing, I can let them be, and take care of myself.

I can turn my headphones on and dance by myself in the kitchen while making dinner, and my mood can instantly change from feeling annoyed to feeling amazing. And not always, but often enough, all it takes is my headphones, and the music.

There were several good things that came out of the pandemic for me. When the choices were so limited for what was available for "fun," music made such a huge difference in enjoying my evening, and was instrumental in changing the feeling of being claustrophobic and annoyed to feeling good.

To get a little deeper than the news or a bad day, another reason I rely on music is because it's naturally healing. Humans have used music, with voices or instruments, across cultures and time. From chanting "Ohm" to drumming with your hands, sounds, notes, beats, and rhythm have an effect on us. We can feel it when we hear it. We instinctively tune in. Even other sounds that are not musical without any particular rhythm like those heard in nature can lull us into a peaceful mindset if we tune in. Listening to birds chirping, wind blowing, or the lulling sound of rolling ocean waves can all have a calming effect.

Another example is a sound bath which can be best described as "sound meditation." Sometimes a sound bath involves some light yoga first, sometimes people use Tibetan bowls or other instruments, and sometimes people chant or use sounds with their voice to soothe and relax the people who are getting "bathed" in the sounds. At one of the sound baths I attended, they were describing how notes and sounds affect water. And because our bodies average about 60% water, that's why we feel the effect as well.

There are many types of sound baths, but the one thing in common is that they use sound for healing. Laying on a yoga mat with beautiful sounds all around feels magical! You can't walk out afterwards without feeling lighter.

Just like the weather can change your mood and your whole outlook for the day, music can be a game-changer. And you don't have to wait for Mother Nature or anyone else to cooperate. So listen to music as soon as you get that feeling that you're "over it" or you need a lift. And if your people, or random strangers, or the traffic, or something else are getting on your nerves, or there's too much noise from the television or too many conversations, and you can't escape your house, or your car, or the situation-put on your headphones. You'll immediately create your own space, just like that. Boom. Or Ohm. Or both.

MEDITATION

Without a doubt, my most important daily mindset habit is my meditation practice. I do Transcendental Meditation (TM) twice a day, every day. I have since the summer of 2000. It was a birthday gift I gave myself when I turned 30, and it's the best money I've ever spent in my life. I honestly don't know what I'd do, or who I'd be, if I didn't have my twice daily twenty minute meditation practice. It's been invaluable to me in so many ways over the years.

I've always considered myself more spiritual (open to different teachings and philosophies) than a follower of any one religion. But some readers might be religious. Know that TM can be done by anyone who believes in any religion-or in none at all. Even if meditation sounds like something you'd like to try, you might think that you could never find the time to meditate. But on a busy day, just like exercise, a regular meditation practice actually gives you the energy and mindset you need to get through it all. To paraphrase the founder of TM, Maharishi Mahesh Yogi: You find a table every day to eat; you find a bed every day to sleep; find a chair, and meditate. And believe it or not but it really is that simple.

If you've spent 20 minutes or more browsing on social media or online shopping or any other distracting thing, then you CAN find 20 minutes to meditate if you want to. Anyone can. You can get up a little early and sit up in bed right where you are and do it. It's such a great way to start the day, whether you're a morning person or not. And I'm not. And that's precisely why I like it in the morning. It helps me ease into my day gently and on the right foot. And then I simply pick another time in the evening to have 20 minutes to sit, and just...be.

My meditations generally feel similar to that first glass of wine but without the calories, without the sugar, and most importantly, without the need for anything else (like another glass of wine which inevitably I always crave after the first glass). To me, meditation is pure contentment.

Even if meditating began for me with how good it felt, it has endured because I know I'm getting benefits far beyond the wonderful feeling. If I could sum it up, one of the main benefits of a regular Transcendental Meditation practice is deep, transformative rest. It's not trying to do anything or forcing anything, because that certainly wouldn't be restful. Meditation that requires effort is not what this is. "Deep rest" is the easiest way for me to describe it, but it's not the full story. I'm not going to try to fully explain exactly what happens during Transcendental Meditation. I know the benefits experientially, but to try to begin to describe something so simple yet profound would be confusing to you, I'm sure. I'm not a TM instructor nor a quantum physicist, and I'd certainly fuck it all up if I tried to explain in detail everything that happens physiologically. If you are interested in those details, you can go to TM.org to learn more. You can find an instructor and dive deeper into all the benefits TM offers. There are TM centers worldwide. There are many great books to read about TM as well. They are the experts and I defer to them. However I will give you an example of an actual physical experience I had during TM about a year or so after I started.

In 2001, my husband, Jeff, and I were in Bali on vacation. While we were slowly joy-riding on a motorbike through a vast expanse of rice fields just outside of a small village, we were robbed at knifepoint. Jeff was driving, and I was on the back of the bike with my purse draped across one shoulder over to my hip. The other motorbike drove right up beside us, the guy on the back grabbed the purse strap along my back, and started sawing with a knife on the strap across my back while we were both slowly riding side by side. I saw the knife and yelled for Jeff to go while struggling with the front strap of my bag. In hindsight, it's crazy to me that I didn't just take the bag off my body and hand it over. He could have easily stabbed me for trying to hold onto it so tightly. But in the moment it was my instinct to struggle to keep my possessions, despite the fact that I was scared shitless. When Jeff realized what was happening, he took off to the right just as the strap on my purse was sawed through-and we wrecked.

Jeff's passport was in the bag that was taken. The temporary passport he got from the US Embassy is funny now. His arm was in a sling, and he didn't look happy in that photo to say the least. I still giggle when I see that old temporary passport. But at the time it was incredibly traumatic. I ended up with a lot of road rash and stitches from a deep wound on my right arm when a metal bracelet was ripped off in the impact of hitting the ground. That deep wound on my arm hurt so much. It throbbed and throbbed. When I tried to hold it up over my head, when I laid down at night, and when I tried to sleep. It continually throbbed for several days straight. I noticed right away, though, that the only time it wasn't throbbing, the only time I wasn't uncomfortable, and trying pointlessly to adjust myself into some arm position that would stop the constant pressure, was when I was meditating.

For me, that was what Oprah Winfrey calls an "Aha moment." I just "got" how much TM slowed my heart rate, slowed my breathing, and made everything okay for a bit, despite the fact that I was severely beat up mentally and physically.

Coming home and going back to my busy and physically demanding fit modeling schedule right after that trauma also made me appreciate this new tool called TM. I had it within me to help calm myself down and help myself heal in the midst of a busy career. I knew after that experience that TM would be a part of my life forever.

I've had a few other traumatic experiences since. In the spring of 2020, my 4-pound teacup Yorkie was attacked by a large bloodhound that I unsuccessfully tried to fight off twice before receiving help from strangers on the street who came out of their homes because of my screams. Long story short, I don't know how I would have gotten through that experience without TM.

TM helps me feel like a more fully-formed human and better able to deal when those trying times arise by bringing me back to my center. But TM is not just for the (hopefully few and far between) traumatic life events. It's for everyday life, for the busy times, the slow times, and all the ups and downs and twists and turns that life inevitably brings. And the best news is-even if everything IS going perfectly well on any given day-meditation enhances my good mood and my overall sense of wellbeing. It is my wine without the headache.

So for me TM is like brushing my teeth. Twice a day. Every day. TM is one of my most important habits, if not THE most important habit. However, even though TM is MY thing, more than anything I recommend meditation, period. There are free meditation apps. Or you can simply close your eyes and breathe. I know it's a huge departure from our culture of doing and going nonstop. But it's invaluable in so many ways.

So if meditation feels right for you, try it. Because it's good for you, it feels good, and because having a clear head is really the best thing, I think, that you could possibly do for yourself in any situation or time in your life. Meditation can help get you there. Discover for yourself.

ADD A THOUGHT

Another one of my favorite mental wellness habits I like to use is adding a thought. There's probably some proper name for this technique somewhere. But it's what I try to do whenever I'm playing something out in my mind that is counter-productive to my well being or is stressing me out.

Here's the premise. When you hear someone say, "Don't think of a white rabbit" all you can think of is a white rabbit, right? So instead of trying not to think of a particular thought which is nearly impossible, you add another true thought of something that you're thankful for or something that makes you happy. It's about making your thoughts work for you instead of bringing you down.

Make sure you add a thought that is true for you. If the thought, "I feel ugly," runs through your head you can't add a thought of, "I feel beautiful," if you truly don't believe you do. Your mind is pretty smart and can't be tricked like that. But you can add the thought "I don't feel like I look at my best today, but I'm going to look at that picture on my refrigerator of when I was that carefree child. I remember that that person is also inside of me, even if I don't feel great about myself at this moment." Maybe you could eventually upgrade it to add in one thought that is true about yourself with something you don't think is ugly at all-your eyes, your smile, your intelligence, your kindness or whatever part about yourself that you're thankful for.

Or maybe it's not a physical flaw that's bothering you, maybe it's a situation. For example, my husband and I own a restaurant. During the pandemic our business was in "Day-by-day, make-it-work" mode with all the pandemic closures and the resulting economic fallout. So when I felt anxiety about all the changes and what would happen, I repeatedly added the thought, "Trust the process." I believed this thought because we also had another restaurant fail years ago with huge financial setbacks and I now know in hindsight that some great things happened because of those setbacks that would have never happened otherwise. That was an amazing learning experience that changed the course of our lives in so many ways that I'm incredibly grateful for today.

And speaking of the pandemic-that pretty much ended my fit modeling career at 49 years young. The last time I was booked was in early 2020, right before the lock-down. The company I was working for opened back up very slowly and only used 2 models rather than 3-and I was the third. I had hoped initially that they would go back to using 3 fit models and I could continue working into my 50s. However, like many companies, they scaled back significantly and laid off entire departments post lock-down. I could have remained annoyed that my last day as a fit model was yet another thing the pandemic created. Instead I added the thought "Be open to change, and see the perfection." Not working outside of the home became a blessing. I never would have been able to finish this book that I had already been working on for years had I not been locked down. This book became my purpose. And though I had always known that I liked to write, that time was truly when I fell as deeply in love with writing as I am with fashion!

And lastly, I am including a story I wrote in May of 2020 during the pandemic:

My sweet, little dog has been in the hospital for 1 week today (because of the attack I mentioned in the meditation section). *I still don't know when she's coming home to us, and because of Covid we can't see her until she gets out. It's really stretching my patience to say the least. But every time I wonder how long until she comes home and I can give her my love and cuddles in person, I try to think that at least she's coming home! A week ago she only had a 50/50 chance of survival. The fact that she's even coming home is a miracle.* [Update: after a long, stressful, 9-day hospital stay, the 4 pounds of the little fighter that she is made it home to us as good as ever. She even still does her "Happy Egg" dance.]

Depending on what's going on in your life, adding a thought might be incredibly difficult. Especially when you're in the thick of all the emotions that come from witnessing a horrible attack on your beloved pet and feeling powerless to help. Sometimes nothing helps but tears. As a matter of fact, when something bad or sad happens to me, I rarely cry-it-all-out-in-one-sesh. I have waves of sadness that I ride whenever something brings me down. Every wave brings in fresh tears, or big sighs at the very least, along with the sad thought. Because sad feelings have their purpose and can't be rushed, I use that time AFTER the sad wave to add in the additional thought. It helps me to not get overwhelmed with the sadness as it works its way through. Let the tears flow, as they are a good release. But through the tears, keep adding the good thoughts, and see what happens for you.

Adding a thought proactively in the beginning is the reverse of realizing it later in hindsight. It can be an effective tool with any difficult emotion like sadness, anger, impatience, or anxiety. It's like when you're in a traffic jam, and you're pissed off because it's making you late. And then when you get to the end of it, you see a bad car wreck, and you're suddenly thankful that you're safe despite being late. It's a matter of shifting your perspective to make whatever situation you're in work for you right now in the present, regardless of the outcome.

I want to repeat that sentence because I believe it is important: IT'S A MATTER OF SHIFTING YOUR PERSPECTIVE TO MAKE WHATEVER SITUATION YOU'RE IN WORK FOR YOU RIGHT NOW IN THE PRESENT, REGARDLESS OF THE OUTCOME by simply SHIFTING YOUR PERSPECTIVE. I believe that shifting your perspective to a more positive outlook can effectively help create a more desirable outcome. I've seen it happen in my life, anyway. And it can't hurt to try.

In contrast to adding a thought, another idea is to write about the thought that won't leave your mind. Put it down on paper or in a note on your phone. You don't need to dwell on it, because the thought is safe there. It's been put to bed like a child that has too much energy because they are overstimulated or overtired. You can leave the excitable thought safely written down while it "sleeps" until morning.

Whatever you choose, know that you can't control the traffic, or the news, or people, or accidents. But you CAN control yourself and your own thoughts about what's going on. And this awareness can be life-changing!

DON'T COMPARE YOURSELF TO OTHERS

Another wellness and mindset tip is to try your best not to compare yourself to others. Not TO the people you follow on social media, not your friends, not to anyone. If I tried to be exactly like anyone else I'd fail without question. So don't get discouraged if you don't do your "perfect you" like me because- guess what? You won't.

You are here because you have unique gifts and abilities that no one else has. No one can "you" like you can. If you catch yourself comparing yourself to someone, stop. Remember to compare yourself to the you of yesterday instead. Use others for inspiration, but do you!

SMILE

Smile first thing in the morning and right before bedtime. This is simple, straightforward, and a great thing to add into your calendar to remind you to do it every day. You don't even need to think of something to make you smile. Just smile and see what happens. Maybe add in a few extra smiles during the day as well. Smile at some strangers, too. And when you come across someone who inevitably gives you that look like they wonder what the fuck you're smiling at, just smile even bigger. Simple, easy, and fun.

THREE MONTHS MAKES A HABIT

One last piece of advice I can give for overall wellness is this: 3 months makes a habit. I don't remember where I heard it, or if it's conclusive on how long it actually takes for something to become a part of your regular routine, but it has always stuck with me. So if there is anything I want to add to or to eliminate from my life, I make a commitment to do it for 3 months. It's not so long that you can't manage it, but it's long enough to become ingrained in your life.

So try it. Put the start and end dates on your calendar. And see where you land in 3 months.

SUMMARY

Not only do you need to have a toolbox of daily mental health habits, you also need to have tools to use when life gets tricky. Because it will. That's life.

So first become aware of the things that trigger you or cause you stress. Then figure out if there is a way to avoid those things. If they can't be avoided, find a plan to work through it. Consistently use whatever tools you have such as finding a great therapist, leaning on a good friend, crying when you need to, or getting extra sleep.

Or add in any of my favorites: listen to music, meditate, add a new thought to focus on something that you ARE thankful for, lose the comparisons while focusing on your best you, and make a habit out of a smile.

If there is one chapter in this book to read and re-read, it's this one. Because developing a proper mindset is a process. As soon as you think you've got it all figured out, something happens that recalibrates your world. Change will happen. Life's all about how you handle that change.

Along the way, being conscious of YOUR elements of wellness and then carving out time each day for those elements is the secret to help you achieve your overall best version of yourself- wherever you land on your journey through life.

Chapter 10 - **Perfect**

I used to think of perfection as something to achieve-a perfect body, a perfect house, a perfect marriage, a perfect family. None of these things are achievable in the strictest sense. But knowing your self-worth and the ability to appreciate the journey IS achievable.

I also used to think of perfection as a destination. A goal. A place to arrive, filled with nothing but carefree contentment at all times. It's not. Life isn't stagnant. Things are always changing. Perfection isn't something to achieve as an end goal. But flowing with the current instead of fighting against it IS achievable.

During those times when you inevitably land in a place of discontent, learn to appreciate your unique journey as a part of the process. Expect to be uncomfortable at times, because our paths are not linear. Rather, we all experience an evolution of twists and turns and ups and downs. Each win is something to celebrate. But when you're not winning, think of the times you've had setbacks and later discovered weeks, months or years later the reason why the setback occurred. Each setback is a part of growth and is an important part of the process-just like the wins.

Therefore the secret to finding your perfect is to SEE THE PERFECTION in everything, including-and especially-IN OURSELVES (which is often the harder part).

By learning to appreciate each part of the process within your nutrition, fitness, and wellness journey, even when you don't fully comprehend it at the moment), you find your perfect. And this appreciation can become your FREEDOM from TRYING to BE or to LOOK perfect.

So please don't beat yourself up anymore for anything you think you do that is less than perfect. Simply become aware-without judgment-of the things that don't seem to work, and move towards things that do.

As I've shared throughout this book, I believe that paying attention to how something makes you feel is the best way to know what works and what doesn't. The answers to our questions of how we feel is our natural inner guide. For example, how does what you eat and drink make you feel? How does your physical activity (or lack thereof) make you feel? How does your state of mind feel? Be honest about the answers. And remember that you can change any behavior that doesn't serve you anymore, starting with awareness. Focus on one thing, and pay attention to not only how you're feeling but to how you WANT to feel. Be specific. Write it down. Then go back to that chapter, re-read it, and use all the additional resources I've provided to dive as deep as you can. Then CHOOSE to CONSISTENTLY do those things that bring you closer and closer to the way you DO want to feel. Repeat these steps for the next thing you want to work on, and so on. The goal is that at the end of most days (though not all, because there will always be growth and challenges), but more often than not, as your head hits your pillow on your luxurious silk pillowcase, you go to sleep feeling good about your choices.

And when you find yourself firmly planted where you want to be, that's when it gets even better. Because you can then turn the focus outwards to others: "How do YOU feel?" and "How can I help?" You can give whatever your gifts are to the world around you in whatever unique way that only you can share-a ripple effect multiplying and magnifying all the good you create from deep within the center of your perfect.

I wish you all the best on your journey. Always remember... you're perfect.

PART TWO:
THE FIT MODEL MANUAL

This portion of the book contains everything I've learned about the business while working with many different clothing manufacturers, including some of the biggest fashion companies in the United States. If you're interested in a career fit modeling, it's time to get technical.

FIT MODELING 101

The following are the common questions aspiring fit models ask. I answer these in the sections below.

Is fit modeling glamorous?

What happens during a fitting?

Who is a good fit model?

How often are you measured?

Is your shape important?

What about cosmetic surgery?

Who books you?

How do you get booked?

How much money do you make?

Do you need a contract?

Freelance, agency, or employment?

Where is the work?

Is fit modeling glamorous?

I have had glamorous moments. I've flown on corporate jets. I've traveled first class to places like Hong Kong, Korea, Taiwan, and Mexico. And I've regularly traversed between New York City and Los Angeles. I've been chauffeured from airports to hotels in Rolls Royces. I've dined out at all the best restaurants in all the cities I've visited. I've drunk champagne while surrounded by fabulous fashion people and looking out at the skyline from the pool deck of 5-star hotels around the world.

So yes there have been glamorous moments. But no, being a fit model is not a glamorous job. You stand for hours. Add in high heels to the mix (which are sometimes though thankfully not often required), and it's even more difficult. People stare at the minute details of the garment you're wearing that most likely doesn't fit well, unless it's in the final approval stages. You have people up close in your personal space pinning and cutting the garment. Therefore people are touching you. Everywhere. Because the hardest parts to fit are around curves.

However, even though for the most part it's not what I would call glamorous, if you're as into fashion as I am, fit modeling can definitely be fun-in addition to the hard work. In fact my experiences throughout the years have led me to believe that it's one of the best relatively unknown careers there are.

The important thing to remember, however, is that modeling is a job. And those that understand that it's not just sitting there looking pretty, those who are realistic about which market they belong in, and those who do their job well are the ones who work.

What happens during a fitting?

Fit models may work closely with these three departments: pattern making, designing, and merchandising. They may work with all three of them at the same time or with just one. It depends on the company and at which stage the garment is in-development or production.

In general, the garments are fit by designers in the development phase. The garments are ready for fitting for production when the designers are finished with the design prototypes for a new season's line. The designers hand these prototype garments off to the technical department to fit the garments for mass production.

The technical coordinators understand the science/math behind how garments are constructed. They cut and pin the garments on fit models until the garment fits well throughout the fitting process. During fittings, it is the fit model's responsibility to make comments about how the garment fits and feels in order to ensure movement and comfort. After each fit session, the technical coordinators communicate the changes to the factory, where those changes are then translated into a pattern.

When a style sells well and the merchants would like to order more of the same style, this often means that they need to duplicate the style in another factory which is called "dual sourcing." The new factory will submit a sample with the goal to make it match identically to the already-approved garment that is selling in the store. This is when the technical coordinators break out their washable markers. The fit model puts on the approved garment from the original factory. The technical coordinators then use the markers directly on the model's skin

118 — Heather Mathes

to mark the garment's neckline, sleeve length, dress length, and any cut-out details. The fit model then puts on the new sample to see if it matches the original. The technical coordinators communicate any necessary changes with the new factory. And this becomes the fit prototype that will be the standard for hundreds or thousands of garments that will eventually be sold in a store near you.

I personally love the whole process of fittings. I generally make mental notes for myself of what I want to buy when it hits the store. The clients usually love to learn what you would buy if you were out shopping at their store. However if you wouldn't be caught dead in whatever you're fitting you might want to wait to be asked rather than shout it out. Someone along the fashion chain likes something about that garment or it wouldn't have ended up in the room for a fitting. But if asked, be honest. Say it in a nice way like, "It's not my personal style or color," or "I'm unsure of where I'd wear that," rather than as saying, "I hate it," or "Hell to the no."

Who is a good fit model?

Outside of specific body measurements, here are the main attributes of a career fit model:

1. *Has the ability to maintain measurements.* You need to have the right measurements, the right shape, the right proportions, good posture, professionalism, stamina, and, most importantly, the ability to maintain your measurements. I have known models under contract who have been sent home due to their measurements being off. So I'll repeat that point: the number one

attribute of a successful fit model, outside of hitting exact measurements provided by the retail clothing company, is the ability to MAINTAIN those measurements over time, which is often the more difficult challenge. Remember from part one that tolerance allows for areas on the body that are slightly bigger and smaller than the specifications of the form. You can also have a few numbers outside of tolerance, and depending on which area of your body those are, that may still work. But in general the majority of your measurements have to be within tolerance. Maintaining exact measurements within a quarter of an inch plus or minus takes a person with discipline and knowledge around nutrition and fitness. Your body becomes your work, and it must be treated as such. Your consistency with your nutrition and workout is as much a part of your job as actually showing up for work.

2. *Works with a company that complements their natural size.* None of this "within tolerance" information means that you need to be rail thin. There are all types of fit models. The traditionally thin modeling world has finally opened up to so many more body types. However, you need to know your natural size. Then you need to find a company that uses that size as its base standard. Looking into those companies that have clothes that seem to fit you well would be a good start. It's about knowing your measurements and finding a company that needs your size, not trying to fit into whatever size you think they need. Remember that if you're not eating properly for your body type, you will not be able to maintain those measurements over time.

3. *Has a physical appearance of "your best you."* While physical beauty (which is subjective) is not technically required to become a fit model, the image of being healthy is important. Although the potential client will want to see their garments on the aspirational consumer they are targeting to buy their clothes, your "look" (and being photogenic) isn't absolutely necessary. It is helpful to be well-groomed and to look the part of your client's target market. A clean, fresh, natural face with minimal makeup is the face you want to present when going on castings for any modeling job. If you can be both the muse and have the right measurements for your client, all the better. But your body measurements and shape are what's most important in fit modeling.

4. *Has experience (an added bonus).* The goal in fit modeling is to produce the best-fitting garment possible. But at the end of the day when up against production deadlines, the goal becomes a commercially saleable garment. An experienced fit model will know which types of fit issues to call out (or not) based on the production timeline of the garment. This type of knowledge from a fit model is beneficial to a company and is desired when hiring a fit model. Knowing how to "move" and "sell" a garment also helps. Therefore, some experience in print, runway, or other forms of modeling prior to fit modeling is an added plus. Experience comes with age, which in fit modeling is not as big of a factor, as long as your measurements are on target and your body is well-maintained.

5. *Is self-confident.* We all have insecurities. But in this career you will need to check your insecurities about your body at the door. As a fit model, clients will compare your body shape and measurements to other models, to the mannequin they use as well as to the industry standard. If you're triggered by it you won't last long. Be objective, realistic, and self-confident. Standing firmly and proudly in "your perfect" is a must.

6. *Has professionalism.* A fit model needs to maintain a professional attitude. All of my main accounts throughout the years have booked me repeatedly because of the professional relationships I had developed. In addition to my fit modeling contracts, I have worked with many of the same print clients for years because they knew I was dependable and reliable. It was therefore easy to keep booking me. (I still occasionally connect with my agency in New York to maintain that professional relationship, even though I haven't worked with them since I had my son.) And this should go without saying, but in addition to being reliable and on-spec, simply being a nice person to be around can help you keep whatever jobs you book. So keep the bitchy attitude at home. Be on time, well-nourished, well-rested, and cultivate a positive and professional mindset within to make yourself easy to rehire.

How often do you get measured?

Fit models are measured on an ongoing basis to ensure they are staying within the desired specifications for that brand. Someone who shows an ability to hit the required specifications over time may get the privilege of being measured on a less regular basis while someone who historically does not hit their body measurement targets may be measured on an even more regular basis. If the model continues to have trouble staying consistent with their measurements it could lead to termination of their position.

Getting measured by the company you are working for is an important part of the job. But you should also learn to measure yourself with a measuring tape on a regular basis as well. It's not as accurate to measure yourself, because you have to lean a bit here and there, so you're therefore not standing up straight or perfectly still. But it's close enough to check in to know you're on spec. If you're not on spec, for example, if you just had the flu and are down several pounds but no one has measured you that day, call it out when you arrive at work so that they can adjust their corrections accordingly.

The most important thing while checking in with the measuring tape, is to always make sure you're eating healthy for your body creating consistency for the client and-more importantly-for yourself.

Is your shape important?

In addition to actual measurements, your natural body shape is important. Some aspects of your shape can be altered with working out-though not excessively or obsessively. There are some exercises that can be done to get slightly bigger or smaller on certain areas of your body. But other parts of your body are simply what Mother Nature gave you. It's important to have realistic expectations for what can be slightly altered and what you are naturally.

Your shoulder slope for example has to have a specific shape. Some companies like more angled shoulders, some prefer shoulders that are more square. And, like everything that is perfectly imperfect about you, your shoulders are probably slightly asymmetrical from left to right. Unless you're ambidextrous, you favor one hand. That means you carry heavy things around on one side more than the other, and one shoulder gets higher than the other. It's okay. Just know which shoulder is closer to the form's slope, and try to switch shoulders if you carry a large, heavy purse around. Better yet, start using a backpack or a rolling bag for lugging around heavy things.

Your shoulder slope is an example of something that you can't change-the angle is what it is. But at the same time you can slightly minimize the asymmetry by being mindful of how you carry things. To minimize is not to eliminate. You don't need to be exact from left to right-and you won't be. One foot is probably slightly larger than the other and one calf is maybe a "hair" bigger (even if it is freshly shaven). That's what makes us human and not carbon copies.

Another shape difference between companies is in the waist-to-hip ratio. Some companies like a higher waist-to-hip measurement ratio than others. That will mean the model will be more curvy or more straight through the waist and hips. You can do some weight training to create a bit more or less curve, but (assuming you're at the right weight for your body), you can't change your waist-to-hip ratio significantly.

Whatever your differences are, what's important is to learn how to speak about your differences to the mannequin form, and to other models the company may be using for fit modeling. This is what professional fit models do-speak to their body shape and measurements as statements of fact for the technical team to use to perfect the fit of their clothing line before it goes into mass production.

What about cosmetic surgery?

It's always your choice how you would like to look. However, know that looking "worked on" is not what the companies that I've worked with have wanted. Most companies (including lingerie) will want a natural shape. They most likely need you to be what most women are rather than a more unrealistic aspiration. And regardless of what they want, you'd have to ask yourself if it's worth risking your health going under the knife for a job.

Elective surgery to change my shape is a risk that up to this point I personally haven't been willing to take. I have always worn padded bras to get the 34 ½" measurement that a size 6 requires. And a bra strap tightening is a simple fix to hike up the apex (the fullest point of the bust) when it gets lower after pregnancy and nursing or with age. You can also buy padded panties to get a bigger bum. I had to do this coming back to fit modeling in my 40s. Seeing myself with the big, round ass I'd never had while looking at my profile in the fitting rooms'

3-way mirror was fun to see for a change. I'd never been so curvy in my life. Check out lovemybubbles.com for more information about padded underwear if you're interested.

Fun props aside, if you do want to explore elective surgery, that is for you to decide for your body without any judgment from others or towards yourself. It doesn't mean you're flawed or that you flunked self-acceptance. You don't have to forgo any type of outer self-care to fully accept yourself as you are. You just need to be absolutely clear about the risks involved, as well as the fact that you can't start from the outside-because that is what doesn't work. It's the opposite. There are so many ways to feel good about yourself. But they all START from the inside.

Bottom line: nobody is living in your skin, and it's 100% your choice how you want to look. But don't ever feel pressured to conform to a shape that isn't naturally attainable in this job or in life itself.

Who books you?

It varies between companies, but in general it's the technical team who most often decide who gets booked. This may include the patternmaker, the technical director, managers, and technical coordinators. The tech team will measure you initially and look at your body in comparison to their standard form to see if you have the same basic shape.

Another person who can book the fit model is the designer. They would most likely choose the fit model that best represents the vision he or she has in mind. In this case, your "look" would help book the job, and exact measurements may be secondary.

The merchant (or buyer) views the clothes that the designer and tech team create together. They choose which items best fit their line by evaluating which colors, prints, fabrics, etc they predict the consumer will buy. They are the fashion-predictors and the number-crunchers, since the bottom line is about sales volume leading to high profit margins. However they only occasionally ook the fit models directly.

How do you get booked?

There is a traditional approach of becoming a fit model, a non-traditional approach, and then there is also "being discovered."

The traditional approach to becoming a fit model involves signing with a modeling agency. You can start by calling local modeling agencies to ask if they are accepting new talent. They will often have open model calls where you can stop in and speak to a representative. When you call, make sure to ask the receptionist what is required to bring to the open call.

If you are a good fit for that agency, they will have you sign a contract as a representative of that modeling agency. The agency will then submit you for potential bookings based on your interests and what the agency recommends you pursue based on your look, talent, or experience. If you are chosen for a booking, all communication about the booking including your pay will come through the modeling agency. The company you are fit modeling for will pay the agency, the agency will keep their cut, and you will get a percentage of the hourly or day rate.

A non-traditional approach to becoming a fit model is to call the corporate headquarters of the clothing retail brands in your area directly. When you call, ask to be connected to Human Resources. They can share what the fit model measurements are for the brand. Ask if they are actively looking for fit model candidates. The answer is almost certainly going to be YES, because they are always looking. Finding a good fit model with the right measurements, the right body shape, is consistent, and professional is not as easy as you might think. In the span of approximately 3 decades of modeling at Express (one of my main clients throughout the years) there have only been 6 total female fit models and only 2 long-term male fit models.

In addition to the traditional or non-traditional approaches to becoming a fit model, some people are "discovered." Someone who is just the right fit and shape who happens to be in the right place at the right time (like being scouted while shopping at a particular store, for example) might be approached when the retail clothing company is looking for another fit model for their brand.

How much money do you make?

Most women with modeling aspirations believe you have to be in editorials to make all the money. Not true. There is a ton of money to be made outside of print work in many types of modeling including runway, showroom and fit modeling. Fit modeling generally provides more longevity than editorials or runway-assuming one stays fit and has the right measurements and proportions for a retailer. This longevity enables the model to potentially make even more money over time.

The typical industry wages can run from $50 per hour to $400 per hour. It depends on who you're working for, what city you're in, and your experience in fit modeling.

Sometimes the younger or newer fit models don't make as much as the older or more experienced ones. This might be due to an inability to provide accurate feedback or to being unproven as to whether they can maintain their measurements. An experienced fit model who communicates valuable comments on the way garments should fit and how garments should feel and can maintain their measurements, gets paid accordingly. Fit models with experience are also the ones who usually have one or several consistent clients they work with. Once a fit model is known throughout the industry to have a good shape, stays consistent, is professional and has a good attitude, she will most likely be booked regularly and can expect to be paid more.

The higher you set your rate in the beginning the better, since it can be harder to bring it up after you or your agency negotiates it. But if you're brand new you do need to get your foot in the door, so going for the lower ranges is fine until you gain some experience. If you're friendly enough with the other fit models you work alongside, ask to have a rate discussion with them. If you're both working for the same company or companies, it's an option to try to raise your rate together, like a union would do, to ensure to maximize your rate as well as make sure you're not pricing yourself out of the job.

When dealing with direct booklins (in all types of modeling), it helps to be a good negotiator. Also, for every day-rate (8 hours of work) booked, it is worth trying to get double time for every hour over those 8 hours. This is important, because fit modeling for over 8 hours is hard to do-even with plenty of breaks scheduled in-and you should be paid accordingly.

You will submit invoices to your agency or to the client directly. They will pay you per job, per week, or per month depending on how much you are working with them.

Since this is a career that may be short-lived due to any number of reasons, treat your career like you're a sports star: get as much as you can, while you can. And, if you're making enough to warrant it, consider getting disability insurance. Because you're self-employed, you only make money if you can show up for the job.

Lastly, something that can sometimes be negotiated is a discount for shopping! It doesn't happen often, but it's worth checking.

Do you need a contract?

Usually the bigger companies will offer you one if you're going to be working with them regularly. I've had multiple contracts, and most of them were independent/freelance though several contracts have been through agencies in New York and the Midwest.

Contracts benefit both the fit model and the client by creating consistency for all concerned. No company wants to fit on hundreds of different models with different shapes and proportions, because it would be challenging to get a garment approved for mass production. The models they fit on must be as close to their form as possible to be able to approve the garment on the model. A contract can help make sure the model they want is available to them.

The contacts can be short (several months) or longer (a year) and are usually renewed if all is going well. At renewal time you can always discuss raising your rate.

Freelance, agency or employment?

I started modeling without an agency, as an independent subcontractor. I have enjoyed the freedom, flexibility, and higher rate this route offers. I have worked with fit models who are direct employees of the company they fit for who generally have a more 9-to-5 schedule but make less money per hour than the independent/freelance route. There are benefits to being an employee such as insurance and stability, but the hourly rate may end up being significantly less. Again, it's just weighing what works best for your own personal situation out of the options offered to you.

If you have an agency (a must in a larger market like NYC or LA), they will do all the negotiating for you. An agency can take a lot of the guesswork and hassle out of it for you and can guide you along. In 2006 I signed with State Management (formerly Model Service Agency) in New York. They helped me navigate the New York market and helped me get clients like Castle Star and Edun. They were invaluable in a market as large as New York. The main thing to consider is what market you are in to determine which approach is better.

The agency will charge both you and your client a percentage of your wages. They should not charge you exorbitant fees for classes or photos if they truly think you have the potential to work. They will point you towards a good photographer for initial photographs which they will use to promote you. They should be able to suggest someone within your budget. Sometimes they will pay for photos upfront for you and then will take it out of your wages after you've booked jobs. Ask if this is an option if they don't offer it.

Where is the work?

Aside from the NYC, LA, Chicago and Miami markets, you have to be in the cities where fashion company headquarters are located. Currently Columbus, Ohio is home to Express, Upwest, Abercrombie & Fitch, Hollister, Lane Bryant, and Victoria's Secret; The Gap and Old Navy are in San Francisco; White House Black Market is in Fort Myers, Florida to name but a few. Do your research and find out if one of your favorite stores that has clothes that fit you well is headquartered nearby.

Congratulations! You're officially a graduate of Fit Modeling 101. However, I still have a bit more to share with you that may help you navigate the world of fast fashion. Next, I'll explain exactly how I came to be a fit model as well as some things I've learned along the way while growing up in this business.

BREAKING INTO THE BUSINESS

I was already modeling occasionally when I got my "big break" into modeling as a career. I had been sent on an audition by an agency to a production company for a different job than the one I ended up getting while I was there. While I was sitting in the waiting room, JoAnn Davis (who booked all the Schottenstein and Value City print and TV commercials at the time) saw me, glanced at my portfolio, and got my information. I wasn't signed exclusively with the agency that sent me for the other audition (which I didn't book), so I took the Schottenstein booking directly as a freelance model. Then they ended up booking me regularly for years to come.

From there I networked with all the other models that regularly worked for Schottenstein's and Value City. They helped me find the clients I could potentially work with, and I contacted those clients directly. Without the help of the other models that were already in the business, I would have never made it without an agency. It's funny, because people usually think of this industry as cut-throat and competitive and that models are bitchy. And though certain people do behave that way, I have had many more positive, beautiful experiences with other models, most of whom I'm still friends with to this day.

Once I had an "in" with the bookers within the Limited Brands, which at that time included Victoria's Secret, Abercrombie, The Limited, and Express, I started working regularly with all those divisions. I was booked for showroom meetings as well as runway for their in-house fashion shows. I also did print for Express for their first online campaign in the 90s, back when the internet was brand new (which gives you some idea how long I've been at this).

My career became lucrative enough to model full time. I had been working with Express for several years before getting randomly pulled aside by the technical team, measured, and "discovered" as a fit model. Being in the business, I knew what a fit model was. I just didn't know that I was "it." I didn't seek it out-it just happened. Those initial measuring sessions led to getting my first fit modeling contract with Express in 1996 which lasted 10 consecutive years, from my mid-20s to mid-30s. And eventually, I'd even come back to fit modeling in 2016 in my mid-40s.

So that's it. My big break was the initial booking sitting in that waiting room. That started off my career with a more traditional modeling background doing print, showroom and runway. That led to the contacts that helped me to randomly fall into fit modeling. Despite the fact that I was already modeling, I would have never known about my potential to become a fit model if I hadn't been in the right place, at the right time, with the right measurements.

The moral of my story is, keep your eyes open for opportunities everywhere. And KEEP NETWORKING with everyone who crosses your path so that even if you don't land that initial booking, you'll be ready when an even better option than you've ever dreamed of opens up to you.

SPEAK UP

So you've done it. You've booked your first modeling job, and you're so excited to start your career. You have the body. But first, before you can continue, you need to find your voice.

When you go on castings or get booked for a job, you wear what they want you to wear. You're the muse. So when you're asked to model something low-cut, high-cut, see-through, or with cutouts, it is important to know what you are, and are not comfortable with, and what you will, and won't do.

Just as importantly, you need to be able to communicate your boundaries with the people who are booking you, prior to entering this business.

The unfortunate truth is that even while being crystal clear about your boundaries you still might have to deal with sexual predators simply because you're a model. Some of these people might think that because you don't have a problem with modeling lingerie or because you aren't shy about your body in any way that it's an invitation for a proposition. An unknown author explained it this way: "No, she's not a slut, you just think like a rapist." Women can wear or NOT wear whatever they want; women can express themselves however they feel sexy and empowered; and women can choose to be in any career they want including modeling and it's NOT an invitation for sex.

I started modeling in the late 1980s. I worked in an era where young models weren't as protected as they are now. And even now, we still have quite a ways to go until young women feel their true worth and are able to speak up for themselves. So yes, I have of course dealt with being hit on while modeling. I mean it was the 90s. Men felt more entitled back then overall. It was nothing that I felt like I couldn't handle. I didn't feel the pressure someone experiences when they think their job or their position is in jeopardy. I just laughed it off at the time and looked at it as harmless. Looking back, I should have said something, should have explained how inappropriate it was, or better yet, should have taken the issue to human resources. But laughing it off was the easy way to dismiss it at the time. The 90s way.

I have modeled for lingerie companies and attended meetings with dozens of people where I've walked around wearing nothing but a sheer bra and thong underwear. I have dressed and undressed in front of too many people to count, both men and women. People I worked with saw my body in different states of undress regularly, so it really wasn't that impressive. But most importantly I felt comfortable, and I was in a SAFE environment.

Occasionally I noticed that some men were shy and looked away when I changed. Women who were brand new to the fashion industry were the opposite in that they often checked me out at every angle until they got used to it. I think they thought it was strange at first for me NOT to be self-conscious. Everyone else didn't really seem to care.

Obviously I'm not modest. Or if I was, I lost any sense of shyness about my body before I even started fit modeling due to changing my clothes at breakneck speed in fashion shows in front of everyone backstage. (And to be honest, I am kind of a nudist at heart. I believe the human body is beautiful in all of its shapes and sizes. I'm of the mindset that we should be seeing more natural, naked bodies and less violence on TV. And don't get me started on nursing moms. That should be normalized. But I digress.)

I wore a bra and panties while changing in fit modeling sessions, so I wasn't completely nude. And again I trusted and liked most of the people I worked with. I felt safe. That's key. The feeling of being safe. Always trust your gut. You know when something feels off. Honor that feeling.

Being married for most of my modeling career also helped. Right at the start at 20 years old I was living with my then-boyfriend whom I married when I was 23, right out of college. I definitely felt safer with that ring on my finger. I was truly fortunate that I was around good people the majority of the time—-though not all models are so lucky. Many of my single girlfriends didn't have the "husband excuse" to brush off unwanted advances. Some have horrible stories of dealing with sexual predators. Thankfully that's not my story to tell.

Going forward there is no room for anyone in a position of power, or for anyone period, creating an uncomfortable situation in an industry known for selling sex in advertising. So for any model entering the fashion industry, or for any young person entering any job, know this: there are sexual predators across all different types of corporations and various ladders to climb. Women shouldn't have to deal with those hurdles, but we do. Until we don't, you need to SPEAK UP for yourself! Do not even try to get into this business if you don't think you'd be able to use your voice.

My advice to those with young daughters considering a career in modeling is to either have them wait until they have the emotional maturity to speak up for themselves, or become a "model mom" and be there with them the entire time.

AND TRUST YOUR INSTINCTS. That can't be stressed enough. If any strange alarm bells go off inside you, honor the feeling and don't proceed. Time's up on the days of making jokes about unwanted advances or ignoring them. If anyone tries to take advantage of their position in booking or hiring you, or puts you in any position that feels uncomfortable, remove yourself and call it out to the human resources department and your agent immediately. And know that if someone wants to hire you because of your look or your measurements, they will.

If they hang sex over your head as an option to take you further, they most likely aren't even interested in booking you. Get away from those people and those jobs. Find another way.

30+ YEARS OF MODELING

Without a doubt, if you consistently focus on ways to create space for consistent self care starting from a young age, you are much more likely to have longevity in this industry. Hopefully, by incorporating some of what you've read throughout this book, you are now aware that regardless of modeling, you have the capability to be at your perfect, natural size at any age or stage of life. The exception of course, is getting pregnant.

If your career lasts longer than the norm, you may wonder when the right time to start a family would be. There is no right answer. And sometimes despite the best laid plans, fate intervenes nonetheless. However keep in mind that fit models should only consider getting pregnant either when they are absolutely sure they are ready to leave the business, or they are working with a company that will hire them back. Chances are slim with the latter because most likely your client will need to find someone to replace you while you're gone. But it certainly is possible and worth a conversation prior to getting pregnant. Otherwise, before making that decision, be okay with leaving the industry to become a mom, as well as following any other passions you want to explore.

In my case, I was comfortable waiting until I felt 100% ready to say goodbye forever to modeling and officially retire. I re-read a book called *Taking Charge Of Your Fertility* by Toni Weschler. I recommend it for women of all ages. Because of this book, I knew my ovulation cycle well. I had already been modeling for 20 years, fit modeling under contract for 12 years, and married for 16 years when I got pregnant on the third try. And in 2009, since I was adopted, my only blood relative in the world arrived: my son Luc.

Post-pregnancy I focused as always on food that gave me energy and on workouts that felt good and alleviated as much of my new-mom stress and sleep deprivation as possible. At that time it was light yoga at home several times per week.

My decision was to retire prior to getting pregnant. So I never thought I'd go back to fit modeling until 2016 when I received a phone call that one of my past clients needed another model. Their first question was if I measured the same. It's funny, because I was doing all of the things I have shared throughout this book, which I DON'T DO to be a certain shape or size or to model, but because it's a healthy way to live my life. So I assumed I was close to target specs, but I didn't know if my shape would work. I mean I nursed for 15 months. My apex is without a doubt lower. Gravity is real. Fortunately it's nothing a pushup bra can't handle. I don't mind the stretch marks from pregnancy and my not-so-tight-anymore abs-after all, my belly made me a mom to the best kid ever. However it was slightly jarring to go back to work in my mid-40s with the "mom bod" and be the only person changing in my bra and panties in front of others under bright fluorescent lights. I mean that takes a bit of courage regardless. Going back at 46 took me a minute to get used to.

I believe this kind of confidence, to go back to work at an age that is ancient for modeling, and with additional "flaws" then of my youth, comes with age. That's something I have loved about being an older model. I was fairly confident about my body when I was younger. You have to have at least some self-confidence in this industry. But ironically I am more confident now than I ever was before. I don't look any better. But I do feel better due to continuing to make self-care a high priority. Of course self-care is not only important for longevity in this career but in life itself.

My modeling career has survived the years, not only by consistently making choices to feel my best regardless of the way that makes me look, but also by NOT listening to a society that has repressed views about the roles and value of older women. Past my prime at 50? No. I don't think so. Growing older doesn't have to look or feel like what we've seen. We can create our own rules, and make any age work however we want to. That's what I've done since I started modeling at the age of 18. And it's worked for me so far as I write this over 30 years later.

In summary, I will always be thankful for my decades-long modeling career and I will always love this industry. Because to me, fashion is art. It's a part of self-expression as an individual and as a culture. I love how fashion changes over time and helps to define each decade. So enjoy each moment in this ever-evolving industry and never take "You're too old" or "You're too [insert anything negative...]" seriously.

> Playing dress-up is fun and should be celebrated at ANY SIZE and ANY AGE. Therefore, whether you're just getting started or you've been in this industry for years, the secret to ANY successful modeling career is to NEVER stop having fun with fashion.

PAID TO BE PERFECT

As I've mentioned throughout this book, you don't have to be physically perfect (which is impossible) to be paid to be perfect. In fact, in this industry the "imperfections" you do have will be described, highlighted, and scrutinized in contrast to the "perfect" non-human mannequin form that each company uses as defined by their exact version of perfect. Do NOT internalize these comments of your imperfections as meaning that you are not perfect exactly as you are. The measurements that don't line up are really just differences. Your imperfections make you you. And ironically your imperfections are a distinctive part of your own unique perfect.

You now have all the information you need to start reaching out to modeling agencies or retail clothing companies to get booked, and start making money being paid to be perfect. I wish you all the best, and I hope you enjoy your career as much as I have enjoyed mine.

Always remember: you ARE perfect-whether you are paid for it, or not.

APPENDIX

FOOD CHART

Printable version available on paidtobeperfect.com

True thought: _____

How do I want to feel? _____

C	P	HP	Food	Feeling
☐	☐	☐	_____	_____
☐	☐	☐	_____	_____
☐	☐	☐	_____	_____
☐	☐	☐	_____	_____
☐	☐	☐	_____	_____
☐	☐	☐	_____	_____
☐	☐	☐	_____	_____
☐	☐	☐	_____	_____
☐	☐	☐	_____	_____
☐	☐	☐	_____	_____
☐	☐	☐	_____	_____
☐	☐	☐	_____	_____
☐	☐	☐	_____	_____
☐	☐	☐	_____	_____
☐	☐	☐	_____	_____
☐	☐	☐	_____	_____
☐	☐	☐	_____	_____
☐	☐	☐	_____	_____
☐	☐	☐	_____	_____
☐	☐	☐	_____	_____
☐	☐	☐	_____	_____

SMOOTHIE RECIPE:

1 cup of water or plant milk
1 cup of frozen fruit
1 to 2 tablespoons of chia, hemp or ground flaxseeds
1 scoop of vegan pea protein powder
1 cup of leafy greens
½ stalk of celery or several cucumber slices

Mix together in a blender until smooth.

GINGER LEMON CIDER SHOT:

1 tablespoon of apple cider vinegar
¼ cup lemon juice (½ lemon squeezed)
¼ teaspoon of ground ginger
5 drops of Stevia
3 tablespoons of water

Stir and drink with a straw.

ALMOND/OAT MILK RECIPE:

3 cups water

¼ cup almonds

½ cup old fashioned oats

1 tablespoon of almond or vanilla extract

1 serving of Stevia or a tablespoon of honey

I use an Almond Cow maker to blend the above in minutes creating fresh milk with the pulp separated. (A blender can be used in combination with a nut milk bag instead.) The pulp I save to eat separately either alone or mixed with a scoop of plant protein powder to which I add in a splash of homemade plant milk.

If any of the information I've provided has been helpful, please leave a review wherever you made the purchase. All feedback is welcome and appreciated.

For further information paidtobeperfect.com will be updated with the specific skin care products I use as well as current articles on nutrition, fitness and wellness.

Thank you for reading. Cheers to your perfect!